endorsements

"Brett Ullman's book on parenting is like a bay we recently anchored in while sailing—clear, vital, restoring. Through wisdom, understanding, and gentle humour, Brett invites us to step back and look at key parenting themes today. This is a powerful guidebook for new parents. More than that, it also contains valuable insight and examples to assist 'veteran' parents in growing and improving amidst our rapidly changing culture."

—DR. CARSON PUE
CEO Arrow Leadership
arrowleadership.org

"Brett is powerfully equipping both students and parents with the knowledge and tools they need to protect against the external and internal damage caused by sin or painful circumstances."

—ERIC SAMUEL TIMM
Faith, Speaker, Artist, and Author
www.nooneunderground.com
www.paintinghope.com
www.twitter.com/ericsamueltimm
www.facebook.com/ericsamueltimm

"Brett does a fantastic job bringing to light the current cultural challenges all of us are exposed to. He tackles controversial issues such as sex, music, and the impact of popular media. I appreciate Brett's straightforward approach, which gives clarity to the influences that are permeating our society. This is a must-have book for every individual working or living with children, youth, or young adults."

—CATHY DIENESCH
Parent, Grandparent, Foster Parent

"Filled with wisdom, real-life stories, and practical tips, this book is a must-read for every parent and youth worker. It's also an easy read due to Brett's conversational style and natural inclination toward encouragement and support."

—GROVER BRADFORD
Centre Street Church—Airdrie Regional
Youth & Community Pastor
Calgary, Alberta
www.bit.ly/d64life

"Brett has done an amazing job of capturing the most relevant information, the most important statistics, and his incredible insight into the ever-changing culture that surrounds our young people. This book is a must-read for any parent, regardless of where you are in your parenting journey. It will provoke thought, discussion, and inter-action—the "stuff" that's missing in many parent-child relationships these days. I wish we'd had a resource like this a decade ago, but I'm thankful that it's here now!"

—CHRIS JUDGE
Youth Worker and Leadership Coach
www.elevateleaders.com

"Brett very poignantly reminds us to be the parents God has called us to be... the kind of parents we desperately want to become. Yet somehow in the midst of parenting, family, and battling the tyranny of the urgent, we have lost our focus and forgotten to be intentional about the things that matter most to us. In his book, Brett challenges parents to be present, involved, and faithful not only in our own walk, but in the lives we demonstrate to our kids."

—LEANNE CABRAL
Bringing Faith Home talks

"Brett has taken the time to research these subjects. This book is a real eye-opener and a must-read for parents. As a parent, I sometimes think I have all the answers. What Brett does with this book is open our eyes to the bigger picture, the influences that are shaping our children's lives whether we like it or not. Armed with this information, we can become better, more informed parents. Thank you, Brett, for allowing God to work through you to present this material in a thoughtful, hard-hitting kind of way. I, for one, needed the reality check."

—CHRISTOPHER JOBE
refinersfire67@yahoo.ca

"Brett Ullman is one of the most knowledgeable people I know when it comes to understanding youth culture and its impact on the emerging generation. In this book, he skillfully decodes the messages teens and young adults are exposed to every day and shows us the flip side of what he calls 'the sexy world out there.' His challenge is not to tell us to run and hide, but to know the truth and be part of transforming the society we live and breathe and make our being in."

—ANDY HARRINGTON
Greater Vancouver UFC/Youth Unlimited
Executive Director

media.faith.culture
Parents 101

Brett Ullman
Worlds Apart Series - Book 2

media.faith.culture: Parents 101

Unless otherwise indicated, all Scripture quotations are taken from The Message. Copyright © 1993, 1994, 1995, 1996, 2000, 2001, 2002. Used by permission of NavPress Publishing Group.

Scripture quotations marked KJV are taken from the Holy Bible, King James Version, which is in the public domain. Scripture quotations marked ESV are taken from the Holy Bible, English Standard Version®. Copyright © 2001 by Crossway, a publishing ministry of Good News Publishers. Used by permission. All rights reserved. Scripture quotations marked NIV are taken from the Holy Bible, New International Version®. Copyright © 1973, 1978, 1984 by Biblica, Inc.™ Used by permission of Zondervan. All rights reserved worldwide. Scripture quotations marked NRSV are taken from the Holy Bible: New Revised Standard Version/Division of Christian Education of the National Council of Churches of Christ in the United States of America. Nashville: Thomas Nelson Publishers © 1989. Used by permission. All rights reserved. Scripture quotations marked NLT are taken from the New Living Translation Holy Bible. Copyright © 1996 by Tyndale Charitable Trust. Used by permission of Tyndale House Publishers. Scripture quotations marked ASV are taken from the Holy Bible, American Standard Version, which is in the public domain.

Printed in Canada.

Word Alive Press
131 Cordite Road, Winnipeg, MB R3W 1S1
www.wordalivepress.ca

WORD ALIVE PRESS
Just Write!

Library and Archives Canada Cataloguing in Publication

Ullman, Brett, 1971-
    Media, faith, culture parents 101 / Brett Ullman.

ISBN 978-1-77069-357-9

    1. Christianity and culture. 2. Mass media--Influence.
3. Mass media--Religious aspects--Christianity. 4. Technology--Religious aspects--Christianity. 5. Popular culture--Religious aspects--Christianity. 6. Christian education of children. I. Title.

BR115.C8U56 2011   261.5'2   C2011-905536-8

To all my fellow journeyers who are living life trying to connect their ancient faith to their modern world.

acknowledgements

thanks to my wife Dawn and my children Zoe and Bennett for all their support over the years with the work I do at Worlds Apart. Thanks to Adam Clarke for his dedication and hard work on this project. Thanks to all my Board of Directors, both past (Daniel McKay, Dave Crawford, Scott Trowbridge, James Boyle, Neil Pasher, Rick Britnell) and present (Brian Althouse, Peter Bozanis, James Cabral, Doug Gowdy, Brian Hall, Andrew Malloch, Brian McAuley, Todd Skinner), for helping behind the scenes. I would like to also thank the other people who have been an integral part of the work at Worlds Apart: Geoff and Erin Thompson (3rdglance.com), Jeff Smyth, Caroline Bruckner, Gary Powell, Tracey Paris and many others. I would also like to thank the people who have supported us through prayer and financial support. We could not do this without you.

I would also like to thank my sponsors who support the work that I do. Thanks to Tyndale University, College and Seminary (Tyndale.ca), World Vision (worldvision.ca), Carruthers Creek Community Church (carrutherscreek.ca), and Master's College and Seminary (mcs.edu).

introduction

"There is perhaps nothing worse than reaching the top of the ladder and discovering that you're on the wrong wall."[1]

back in the fall, I had a chance to go to the Leadership Studio at Muskoka Woods Sports Resort in Rosseau, Ontario. I read the following quote on one of the TVs: "A leader is someone who looks at the world and says it doesn't have to be this way. And then does something about it." I personally don't think the world has to be the way it is today.

One of the things I say to the youth I speak to is, "If you think your best years are going to be in high school, I

---

[1] Soccio, Douglas J. *Archetypes of Wisdom: An Introduction to Philosophy*, 7th Edition (Belmont, CA: Wadsworth Publishing, 2009), p. 153.

feel sorry for you." Our lives as adults should be defined by events that have occurred since our senior years in high school. Our lives should not be flashbacks to the good ol' days, but instead to what we continue to do to further God's kingdom on earth. We should always strive to believe that our lives will improve and get better as we move forward and grow through new experiences. We should have the same desire to continue learning and growing so that we can engage the students and children in our lives. We should begin to ask ourselves some tough questions:

- Can we do ministry differently?
- Can we parent our children differently?
- How can we be better Christians?
- How can we be better fathers and mothers?
- How can we be better husbands and wives?
- Can we change our relationships with our spouses?
- Can we change the relationships we have with our kids?

I hope no one begins reading this book thinking they are at the top of their ladder, at the peak of their existence, having arrived at perfection. Simply put, that just isn't the case with any of us. But worse than that would be approaching this book with the thought that you can't change. I hope you don't think you have climbed so high that there is no way to scale back down without hurling yourself off the ladder. That isn't the case, either. We can journey together—a journey of questions and respectable conversation. I hope we can all come in with the mindset that something could change.

Here is the biggest struggle with writing this book: what could I say to make you change anything?

If all I do is write this book, or if I have the opportunity to speak in front of you for a few hours and that's it, what a waste of time writing this book will have been. I'll give you everything I have; all I ask of you is that you allow your heart, mind, and soul to be open to the possibility of change, and more importantly to question.

What should we question? That seems like a perfect place to start because the answer gives us an infinite number of possibilities. We should allow ourselves to question everything around us. Whether it is TV, magazines, movies, or the music we listen to, we should always be asking questions.

What values does the author have?

What do the lyrics say is normal?

Will that t-shirt really change the way people treat me?

These are all questions that will lead us into a world that is conscious of the messages that are all around us every day. Without the possibility of asking questions, the world would be a very boring place with very boring people who only believe what they are told to believe.

What are these messages that we hear all around us?

It's noise! It is the noise that comes from the constant messages being fired at us through our phones, emails, texts, and the many screens that exist in our lives. The noisy messages that are making up our choices, values, and belief systems allow us to do one thing very well—hide. We can hide behind our screens and enter a world that seems enticing and perfect, but it only appears this way because we haven't begun to question what this noise has done to our lives.

In the book *A Tribe Apart*, author Patricia Hirsch states, "Adolescents today inhabit a world largely unknown to adults."[2] That was back in 1998, so we can only imagine that the gap has gotten wider. Parents, you need to take this to heart. Youth workers, you need to communicate this clearly with parents.

Think about it for a second.

What did *you* consciously hide from your parents?

Now, what do you think *your* kids are hiding from you?

Is it their music, what they watch on TV and on the internet, or is it everything they possibly can?

If you work with youth or have kids, realize that the world they inhabit is very different than the one you grew up in. *Macleans*, in their January 2007 issue, made this point clearly when it ran an article entitled "Why Are We Dressing our Daughters like This?" The article was a history lesson of the sexualizing of the schoolgirl look, a look that was changed from school uniform to sexual fantasy because of media influences like manga, Russian literature, and American porn. According to the article, "Before a girl has half a chance to reflect on issues of belonging and desirability, she is being confronted with a market that tells her she should be concerned about this—even when she's as

---

[2] Hersch, Patricia. *A Tribe Apart: A Journey into the Heart of American Adolesence* (New York, NY: Fawcett Columbine, 1998), p. viii.

young as 8."[3] The concern the author is referring to is maturity, not in terms of actions and mentality, but in sexuality. The article goes on to say, "Every message to a preteen girl… says that it's preferable to pose on the beach rather than surf, to shop rather than play, to decorate rather than invent."[4]

This hits home for me because my daughter is nine! My generation didn't have to deal with this when we were growing up. We didn't have magazines calling eight-year-old girls skanks and hookers.

Back when I was teaching, a girl was found at a school near mine giving oral sex for five dollars a pop. The guys were lined up ten deep. We can't even begin to talk about the emotional damage this will inflict later in life. Again, my generation didn't have that. We didn't have girls getting pregnant in Grade Six, but I see this problem now as I travel—girls in Grade Six through Twelve with HIV/AIDS.

Are all young people like that? No, of course not, but the reality is that the world they inhabit is vastly different from anything we ever knew, and today's youth want to keep it that way.

We have taken adolescence and made it small—really small. Take my daughter, who just left her cartoon world behind, for the most part, and is right into dating with shows like *Hannah Montana* and *iCarly*. We don't really have a young childhood anymore. The reality and mentality of many of our young people can be summed up as follows:

---

[3] George, Lianne. "Why Are We Dressing Our Daughters Like This? Eight-year Olds in Fishnets, Padded 'Bralettes' and Thong Panties: Welcome to the Junior Miss Version of Rauch Culture," *Macleans Magazine*, January 1, 2007.
[4] Ibid.

> It used to be that parents protected their kids
> from the hard truths of life. Today teens protect
> their parents. It's a harsh world out there and I
> don't think mom or dad could handle the things
> that I deal with each and every day, so I don't say
> anything. Sharing sex is as casual as giving a
> friend a backrub, and if I'm trying to live my faith
> and live purely, and that is my reality, how do I
> share that with my parents? I don't. I simply let
> them think that things are the same as when they
> were kids.[5]

I also remember the "one swear word" rule in my house when I was growing up. If there was one swear, the show was turned off, but I could continue watching if I looked down the hall and saw that my parents had missed it.

Is this how it works in your homes and ministries?

Why do kids today hide behind their screens? If you said it's probably a feeling of guilt, you're probably on the right track. The feelings of uncertainty they have while watching or listening indicates that they're already questioning themselves internally. That awkward feeling in the pit of their stomachs can sometimes be the coolest part of change, because it happens without our knowledge or probing. It just happens.

Why does it happen?

It happens because something we have just read, watched, or listened to does not agree with what we have determined to be true, noble, or genuinely good. That's why we have the same feeling in the pit of our stomachs

[5] Eller, Suzanne T. *Real Teens, Real Stories, Real Life* (Colorado, CO: Cook Communications Ministries, 2002), p. 13.

when we see violence happen in a movie as we do when we see it close to home. We know that violence, greed, and excessive swearing aren't part of a normal, everyday life. As we begin to question and probe all the noise and screens in our lives, we can make clearer choices on what we allow to influence us.

table of contents

MEDIA

media

et's dive into the media, or the noise that is bombarding us every day. A recent study done by the Kaiser Foundation, called *Generation M2: Media in the Lives of 8- to 18-Year-Olds*, reported the following numbers about the amount of media found in the average household.

> Today the typical 8- to 18-year-old's home contains an average of 3.8 TVs, 2.8 DVD or VCR players, 1 digital video recorder, 2.2 CD players, 2.5 radios, 2 computers, and 2.3 console video game players. Except for radios and CD players, there has been a steady increase in the number of media platforms in young people's homes over the past 10 years (with the advent of the MP3 player, the number of radios and CD players has actually declined in recent years).[6]

---

[6] Rideout, Victoria J., Ulla G. Foehr, Donald F. Roberts and Henry J. Kaiser Family Foundation, *Generation M2: Media in the Lives of 8- to 18-Year-Olds* (Menlo Park, CA: Henry J. Kaiser Family Foundation, 2010).

There was also a huge increase in the amount of time spent enjoying one form of media or another.

> Moreover, given the amount of time they spend using more than one medium at a time, today's youth pack a total of 10 hours and 45 minutes worth of media content into those daily 7½ hours—an increase of almost 2¼ hours of media exposure per day over the past five years.[7]

So, we have a couple of issues that we need to address:

- There's more media devices in their lives than there was in ours, and
- They spend on average two more hours per day engaged in media than our generation did.

What does media mean to you? What is the first thing you think of when you hear the word "media"?

Media is defined by the author David Dark as the "plural for the mediums through which someone or something is getting through (or trying to get through) to us. Let's name a few: letters, billboards, cell phones, novels, songs, newspapers, magazines, television, and emails."[8] I would add video games and movies to that list as well. Media by its very definition is communication, and that is where our questioning begins. We need to question what is being communicated to us, who is doing the

---

[7] Ibid.

[8] Dark, David. *The Sacredness of Questioning Everything* (Grand Rapids, MI: Zondervan, 2009), pp. 95–96.

communicating, and what we are communicating back from what we hear. In other words, how is what we are influenced by influencing those around us?

Let me tell you a story of my first experience with media and its influence.

I was seventeen and I can honestly say this day would turn out to be one of the weirdest days of my life. I was going with my youth group to hear a media talk, much similar to what this book is doing... or at least I thought that's what the night was going to be. Next thing I knew, a man came into the room with some records (you know, the big version of CDs) and played them backwards... all night long. That was it. That was his means of getting his message across to us.

That wasn't the weird part. The weird part came when he finally spoke. He asked us four simple words—"Did you hear that?"

He didn't tell us to listen for anything before he finally came around to speak, and when he did speak no one knew what he was talking about. Instead of a response, he received blank stares and looks of confusion from everyone in the room.

Finally, he told us what we heard—at least, what we were *supposed* to hear. Here is how the next couple of minutes played out.

"It says, go worship Satan," he said.

I said, "Dude, no, it doesn't."

"Yes, it does."

With the simple answer of "Yes, it does," his point was apparently made and he could move on to the next record.

No questioning of the message was allowed, and thus he proved his point, I guess. "Go have sex" was the apparent message of the next backward record, and that was my first experience with media, its influence and message, and how it apparently affects our lives.

What simple answers are we giving the youth around us everyday?

- "...because it's bad."
- "...because I said so."
- "...because your mom said so."

The question we need to ask ourselves as parents and leaders is this: are we telling them what media says, or are we allowing them to honestly question what's right in front of them?

At the end of the night, he was convinced that he had made his point, to which I still said, "No, you didn't." What was his message that night? Christians should not listen to any secular music. To be very honest and blunt, I disagree with the term "secular music," and I completely disagree with the term "Christian music." That night, I was not just told who I could or couldn't listen to, but I was handed a record that was acceptable in his eyes for me to listen to. It was a record by Sandy Patty, and if anyone under the age of twenty-five knows who I'm talking about I'll be surprised. The record was, in his view, good old Christian music that would not lead me astray. Now, my favourite band growing up was Skinny Puppy, a band that

had lyrics ripe with language. They were a far cry from the
Sandy Patty record that had just been placed in my hand.

I look back and think it was funny, but back then it was
far from funny. I took that record with me to the bus, but it
did not make the journey back home with me; I smashed it
on the ground beside the bus. That night held some very
severe consequences for my personal relationship with Jesus.
The Jesus presented to me that night was not a Jesus I
wanted any part of and I did not want to go back. Many
times we are presented with a Jesus who is far from the Jesus
that truly is. As a young kid, the church—and this false
presentation of who God was—turned me off, and it should
not have been that way. The reality of the situation is that
the Jesus we preach is not always the Jesus who is.

There is a danger when we begin to label things
Christian and secular. Rob Bell, in his book *Velvet Elvis*,
responds to our tendency to label things secular and
Christian by pointing out that if we begin to label the
messages coming at us we lose sight of what is acceptable.

> The danger of labeling things 'Christian' is that it
> can lead to our blindly consuming things we have
> been told are safe and acceptable. When we
> turn off this discernment radar, dangerous things
> can happen. We have to test everything. I thank
> God for the many Christians who create and
> write and film and sing. Anybody anywhere who
> is doing all they can to point people to the
> deeper realities of God is doing a beautiful thing.
> But those writers and artists and thinkers and
> singers would all tell you to think long and hard

about what they are saying and doing and
creating. Test it. Probe it.[9]

Questioning the messages in our lives is not a new
concept. Paul would have had to do the same as he travelled
around Greece, learning about the pagan gods and engaging
those within his community in conversation about what he
read and learned along the way. Paul would not have
believed or agreed with all the philosophers and poets he
engaged with throughout Greece, but he questioned
everything that was presented to him.

> In the same way that something can be labeled
> "Christian" and not be true, something can be
> true and not be labeled Christian. Paul quotes
> Cretan prophets and Greek poets. He is
> interested in whether or not what they said is
> true. Now to be able to quote these prophets
> and poets, Paul obviously had to read them. And
> study them. And analyze them. And I'm sure he
> came across all kinds of things in their writings
> that he didn't agree with. So he sifts and sorts
> and separates the light from the dark and then
> claims and quotes parts that are true.[10]

This is my goal for this book, just as it is when I speak—
question everything in your life and look for what has light
and truth and what has darkness and lies. My goal, unlike
the message I received as a teenager, is not to tell you what

[9] Bell, Rob. *Velvet Elvis: Repainting the Christian Faith* (Grand Rapids, MI:
Zondervan, 2005), p. 86.
[10] Ibid., p. 87.

you should or should not listen to or watch at home, but simply a message of questioning. Allow yourself to question the messages that are coming at you, and then decide for yourself what you think the best and most truthful option would be.

Chances are if you're reading this book, you:

- work with youth, or
- are a parent of a youth.

It doesn't matter whether you are a volunteer, paid youth worker, senior pastor, or educator; your goal should be the same—that you take some of these principles back to your church, school, or children.

We can all individually question what we are allowing to influence our lives. I believe it was our generation that first began to really question what we were being told and pushed back at the boundaries that were placed in our lives. For example, I grew up Baptist and as a part of that was told not to drink, smoke, or dance. These boundaries led to us asking a very important question: "Why?"

The response was always the same: "Because."

Each of us should ask the "why" question. If we're not asking that question, we're just being blindly influenced.

Our generation was the one to say, "No, why? Tell me why. Why can't I have one beer?" Well, the Bible tells us not to get drunk. Romans 13:13 says, *"Because we belong to the day, we must live decent lives for all to see. Don't participate in the darkness of wild parties and drunkenness, or in sexual promiscuity and immoral living, or in quarreling and jealousy"* (NLT).

Then finally it was like, "Okay, you can have one beer." Our generation took that freedom and ran with it. The problem was that we went too far, and now we have a growing trend of youth pastors who are drinking heavily and swearing. This does not, of course, describe all youth leaders, but as I travel across North America I see that it's slowly becoming the norm. Hopefully we can look at this material as individuals and integrate these principles in our own lives.

One of the big challenges I face is this: how do we take these principles to the parents of youth? If you're a parent and not a youth worker, you have a head start. If you're a youth worker, I believe the core of youth ministry has to be talking to parents. As youth workers, we can teach them whatever we want, but since they end up going back to their home lives, we have to educate parents.

Blind Lines

I challenge young people, I challenge parents, and I challenge leaders on something as simple as a black line. In the blank space on the next page, draw a single black line down the center of the page.

Okay, now look at your life. That's right, you just illustrated your life in, like, three seconds. It is that easy. This is what we do, though, isn't it? We draw a line in our life and say things like this: "I'll listen to this band, but not that band." How about this: "I'll watch this show, but not that show." We live a life that is separated by the lines we draw. When I ask why items are on one side of the line or another, the responses I hear are always interesting. They are interesting because we often don't know why, or we place them based on what others think or say or how they are perceived through media communication.

The line that confuses me and breaks my heart the most is the line we place in our church lives. We will team up with *this* church, but not *that* church. We exclude churches based on denominational titles, whether it is Baptist, Anglican, Pentecostal, or a community church. We refuse to work with the people down the street because of the title in their church name.

Why is that?

Why are we allowing our pride to dictate church funds?

If it costs money to bring in speakers, run large-scale events, and pay the electric bill, why are we not coming together as a community of God's people for the sake of kingdom building?

Michael Frost, in *Exiles*, states that it is not the single church that builds the kingdom, but a community based in Christ:

> We are called by God to be God's and each other's companions. The term "companion" is rich in meaning, coming from the Latin *com panis* ("with bread"). We are called to deliver on the promise that we will share bread with each other. There are many names for this sharing: utopia, community, the kingdom of God. It is this sharing that Jesus calls us to. He does so in the sacramental feast known as the Lord's Supper. He breaks bread and shares it with us. Indeed he is the bread, the nourishment that binds us together in our mutual need of him.[11]

When was the last time your church broke bread with the church down the street?

The lines we draw between our church and other churches do nothing in terms of kingdom building. Those same lines destroy ministry budgets as we spend money without sharing what God has blessed us with. If your church is blessed with a large budget, start inviting the

---

[11] Frost, Michael. *Exiles: Living Missionally in a Post-Christian Culture.*
(Peabody, MA: Hendrickson Publishers, 2006), p. 16.

church down the road, which might not be so blessed
financially. It's about time we started to break down these
lines so that God's kingdom can flourish.

My favourite object, which is constantly defined by the
lines of what is acceptable and what isn't, is the Bible. Have
you ever had to read your Bible out loud in a group setting
only to have someone look at you with disgust? I have, and
it hurts. Why did this happen? Because I wasn't reading
from the right translation, and this has happened many times
and my response is always the same: "Well, would you like
Greek, Hebrew, or both? What would you like?"

They all want the same thing—the good old King James
Version (the one with the *thous* and the *thus sayith the Lords*).
But don't be discouraged. The Bible was not originally
written in English and the same problems we have with one
translation we have with another. All the English
translations out there have been translated by humans from
the original Greek and Hebrew sources.

Many teenagers have approached me with this same
question: what version of the Bible should I read? Your
parents might say English Standard Version (ESV), your
pastor might be telling you to read New King James
Version (NKJV), and your friends might be telling you to
read The Voice translation because it is new, fresh, and easy
to read. Quite often in our Christian circles we are asked to
draw a thick line when it comes to the Bibles we read. I
have some encouraging news for everyone out there. It
does not have to be this way. I say read whatever
translation, whatever Bible, you have and are comfortable
reading.

I recently read The Voice translation. It was one of the most interesting translations I have ever read in my life. My favourite Bible, however, would be the NASB/The Message Parallel. If you want two different versions at the same time, put these together. I like that. What if we all read every version? Then maybe we could decide which one is the best.

I'll give you an example. There is a video on YouTube of a church in North Carolina that burned many versions of the Bible that were not the King James Version. They also burned many books by leading Christian authors because the church had clearly drawn some very thick and misguided lines when it came to the books they read. Representatives of this church said, "We are burning books that are satanic... Other Christian authors that we consider heretics, such as Billy Graham, Rick Warren..."[12]

The line that church is taking is that these books are okay over here, but those books in the pile are satanic and wrong. The problem is that they are labeling actual *Bibles* as having satanic influence in the world—Bibles such as the New International Version (NIV), The Message, the New King James Version (NKJV), and the American Standard Version (ASV), among others.

Does this line not go against the very nature and source of the Bible?

The Bible is God's word, given to us so that we can establish a relationship with him. The Bible is meant to show us how to gain everlasting life. The lines this North

---

[12] Associated Press, *YouTube*, October 13, 2009, http://www.youtube.com/watch?v=4FkbgeR8LKs (accessed April 5, 2010).

Carolina church is drawing says that certain Bibles don't tell the truth of God's word. The key word is *truth*.

Do you see the danger in drawing lines like that? It is easy to separate things into categories of right or wrong. We begin to separate things into categories so that we can then argue whether or not they are truly right or wrong.

In what areas do you separate things into categories?

I'll watch this show, but not that show.

I'll listen to this artist, but not that artist.

I'll watch *Saw*, but I won't watch *Hostel*.

What do the categories say about what you value as right and wrong?

When we begin to separate things into categories, we usually end up with one of three worldviews based on how we see our role in the world.

The first, and quite honestly the easiest, choice is that we become separatists.[13] We remove ourselves completely from the world, people, society, and culture. The danger is not in the Christian bookstores, Christian camps, or religious schools because in and of themselves these things are not wrong. The problem is when we allow a separatist mindset to invade our whole life.

I once had a Grade Seven student come up to me and say, "Brett, I'm really scared of those people."

"Which people?" I asked. "The Baptists? Who are we talking about here?"

"The non-Christians," the student answered.

---

[13] Oberbrunner, Kary. *The Journey Towards Relevance: Simple Steps for Transforming Your World* (Lake Mary, FL: Relevant Books, 2004).

The sad thing is that this is a typical response from our young people.

When we preach about the evil world and how we must be separate from it, what are we teaching the younger generation? What are we accomplishing when they become afraid of the people around them? Millions of good people all around us just don't know Christ. They're our neighbours, they're at Tim Horton's with us, they're standing beside us when they order at the fast food counter, they're all around us. Michael Frost once again points us towards a solution:

> The problem with all this is the fact that many Christians don't actually go to third places. In fact, as I said earlier, for many Christians the church is their third place. All their leisure time is spent at church meetings or gatherings, belonging to church based communities and occasionally socializing with our church friends. While not-yet Christians are connecting over takeout Thai or whipping up a Moroccan couscous dish or barbecuing Atlantic salmon steaks, Christians are out several nights a week at church services, small groups, and leadership committee meetings. They have no time to engage meaningfully in third places, so the kind of exciting missionary table fellowship that Paul practiced is lost to them.[14]

---

[14] Frost, Michael. *Exiles: Living Missionally in a Post-Christian Culture.* (Peabody, MA: Hendrickson Publishers, 2006), p. 167.

The concept of "third places" is interesting, one which you might have heard about from a young person who works at Starbucks. Starbucks builds their business practices off this concept and makes sure all new employees understand the importance of providing the customer with a "third place."

In his book, *Pour Your Heart Into It: How Starbucks Built a Company One Cup at a Time*, Howard Schultz quotes Ray Oldenburg, a Florida sociologist:

> Without such places, the urban area fails to nourish the kinds of relationships and the diversity of human contact that are the essence of the city. Deprived of these settings, people remain lonely within their crowds.[15]

I've seen friends write, read, meet, and even build relationships with their spouses out of Starbucks locations, and most of them would say that it's because they have the feeling of a "third place." They meet here in community because it's not a home or office; it's a neutral space to enjoy everything around them. The challenge is how we can make the church our "third place" without taking us away from the world at the same time.

Michael Frost switches around this mentality and establishes the church as the *first* place, and that we, as missional Christians, need to get into the third places to reach the people where we feel most comfortable. As

[15] Schultz, Howard and Yang Jones Dori. *Pour Your Heart Into It: How Starbucks Built a Company One Cup at a Time.* (New York, NY: Hyperion, 1997), p. 120.

Christians and parents, we need to make sure that third places are an intentional part of our missional work.

> Third places are the most significant places for Christian mission to occur because in a third place people are more relaxed, less guarded, more open to meaningful conversation and interaction... It's in the third place that we let those guards down. It's here that we allow people to know us more fully. It's here that people are more willing to discuss the core issues of life, death, faith, meaning, and purpose. For example, have you worked with a colleague who you considered to be fairly buttoned-down and straight-laced, until the annual Christmas party, when after a few drinks this person is dancing on the tables and telling uproarious (often dirty) jokes? Or what about the office clown who's always making light of every issue at work, until at a bar after 5.00 pm one Friday this comedian tearfully opens up to you about a personal tragedy? Why? Because there seem to be different rules about the appropriateness of intimate conversation at work than there are in a social context.[16]

Are we as parents and leaders causing our children to lose connection with the world around them? Dan Kimball, in *They Like Jesus But Not the Church*, tackles many of the stereotypes currently plaguing church culture. He points out one issue that ultimately leads to a separatist worldview:

---

[16] Frost, Michael. *Exiles: Living Missionally in a Post-Christian Culture.* (Peabody, MA: Hendrickson Publishers, 2006), p. 56–59.

> Pastors face subtle pressure from Christian
> parents to have good youth programs to make
> sure that their kids stay away from the bad non-
> Christian kids and have the opportunity to meet
> other Christians.[17]

The danger is in the message that is given to the world. Craig Gross and J.R. Mahon, in their book *Starving Jesus,* explain that the danger is that when we completely remove ourselves from culture and society without looking back, we ignore one of Jesus' core values. We no longer have the opportunity to teach the ways of Jesus to those who need it.

> Be in the world, not of it. We love to screw this
> one up. We automatically assume we should
> check out and pay no attention to the pop
> culture radar. Forget about people who are led
> astray. Build a bunker in the backyard, cover our
> kids' eyes and ears, and hope all your willpower
> and energy will be enough for the world to stay
> away. The problem with this behavior is when
> you follow Christ, you will be asked to serve
> those who are of the world.[18]

It's quite easy for us to look at the world around us and say that everything is bad, or even evil. That's an easy choice, because it takes no work at all; we just look around, spotting everything that's against God and do nothing about it. This decision takes no effort or work on our part.

---

[17] Kimball, Dan. *They Like Jesus But Not the Church.* (Grand Rapids, MI: Zondervan, 2007), p. 41.
[18] Gross, Craig and J R Mahon. *Starving Jesus: Off the Pew, Into the World.* (Colorado Springs: David C. Cook, 2007).

God, however, tells us to avoid this type of worldview. *"Live creatively, friends. If someone falls into sin, forgivingly restore him, saving your critical comments for yourself. You might be needing forgiveness before the day's out"* (Galatians 6:1). In essence, God is saying, "Hey, live like me. I forgave, restored, and loved the people of this world, even though I am not of this world."

"And he said unto them, Ye are from beneath; I am from above: ye are of this world; I am not of this world" (John 8:23, KJV). Jesus had every right to live with a separatist view, because he did not sin; he was the only one who could look around at everyone around him and judge them by their sins.

One difference in our lives is pride. We overlook our own sins and judge others. We become too prideful to see our own sin when we condemn others. Here is what the Bible says about that: *"And why beholdest thou the mote that is in thy brother's eye, but considerest not the beam that is in thine own eye?"* (Matthew 7:3, KJV) We can also add this verse: *"If you live squinty-eyed in greed and distrust, your body is a dank cellar. If you pull the blinds on your windows, what a dark life you will have!"* (Matthew 6:23)

Do we notice the speck before the plank?

Jesus had to deal with this sort of thinking all the time in the form of Pharisees. They thought their law and commitment to the Torah (the Books of Moses) would keep them pure and holy. However, they were only separating themselves from everyone else through prideful arrogance. Jesus warned about this mentality in the Gospel of John: *"Ye search the scriptures, because ye think that in them ye have eternal life; and these are they which bear witness of me"* (John 5:39, ASV). In reality, it is easier to follow laws that are written down in a book, like the Ten Commandments, than to follow Jesus' ultimate commandment to love everyone.

> If all you do is love the lovable, do you expect a bonus? Anybody can do that. If you simply say hello to those who greet you, do you expect a medal? Any run-of-the-mill sinner does that. In a word, what I'm saying is, Grow up. You're kingdom subjects. Now live like it. Live out your God-created identity. Live generously and graciously toward others, the way God lives toward you. (Matthew 5:46–48)

Think about how Jesus treated the people of his time. He healed the sick, including the lepers who were outcasts. He sat with the woman at the well, he taught through the Samaritan, and he called the children to him. He loved without marginalizing. Jesus even tells us that oftentimes the world around us won't pollute our lives; it is how we let others influence our worldview. He then called the crowd together and said, *"Listen, and take this to heart. It's not what you swallow that pollutes your life, but what you vomit up"* (Matthew 15:10–11).

We have to ask questions about all the music, violence, and videos that come into our lives, because if we allow them to become our influences we become like the Pharisees. God, at that point, starts to fall away from the center of our lives and media takes center stage in guiding us, just as the Torah and other books of the law did for the Pharisees.

Pastor Chris Seay, from Ecclesia Church in Houston, works through the notion that people and items—in this case, we can add media into the argument—should not be broken down into good and evil. He said that a better way to break these things down is in terms of "shalom" and "not shalom." He goes into more detail in his new book, *The Gospel According to Jesus: A Faith that Restores All Things.*

> Modern Christians have taken a previously integrated world and subdivided it into the sacred or secular, physical or spiritual, good or bad, profane or religious—categories that do not serve us well because they are simply untrue. God created the physical, and that makes it uniquely spiritual. The so-called "bad people" are also created in the image of God.[19]

When we say things are straight-out evil, it conveys the message that the world is irreconcilable with God. God loses his power to reconcile and his authority is called into question. The cross loses its significance. However, if the person or object has "lost" shalom, it can be brought back to God, putting the grace of God into action.

People are not good or bad; they are simply broken, and God has either restored them to shalom or is seeking to restore them to shalom. Imagine seeing people as "shalom" or "broken shalom" rather than good or bad. If you see

---

[19] Seay, Chris. *The Gospel According to Jesus: A Faith that Restores All Things.* (Nashville, TN: Thomas Nelson, 2010), p. 146.

them as broken shalom, you're not allowed to look down on them; instead, you are called to join God in his redemptive work in their lives.[20]

When we start living a separatist worldview, we begin to see the world as irreconcilable to God. The point we need to remember is that when we live in this worldview, we take away the authority of God's word and place the authority on man's laws, which are flawed because of sin.

Our second choice is to become conformists. To conform is to give in to or submit to the rules or authority of something else. When we choose this route, unlike separatists, we turn to society, the world, and culture for all the answers.

Let me tell you about a friend of mine from university who really speaks about the danger of conforming. One day, we went to hang out, just like you are probably going to do later today, when he turned to me and said, "Brett, I want to start living my faith out among my people."

"Your people?" I responded.

At this point, I have come to understand that he is saying that his entire worldview has become an "us vs. them" issue. The great secular vs. Christian divide had shown up in his thoughts. The obstacle in this type of worldview is that the message and words of God can become diluted and, at times, lose their effectiveness.

He responded, "You know, bar people."

So he began going to the bar, sharing his faith when he could with people there, but he was quickly challenged on the Jesus he followed.

---

[20] Ibid., p. 148.

"Why would I need your Jesus?" one of his people challenged him. "You are exactly like me."

There is the danger of conforming completely to society and culture. Jesus in essence becomes just another homeboy (with the t-shirts and trucker hats) whose voice can be seen as a suggestion rather than the authoritative call to restoration it is supposed to be. This has become an issue for so many of us. We want the friendly, loving Jesus, but not the judge-and-jury Jesus. The moment we think our actions and thoughts are beyond judgment, we become unable to hear any criticism towards our own lives. It is the church and other believers who have the ability and calling to become accountability partners in our lives. However, we all know how we react to criticism and questions of accountability in our own lives. They are often reactions of self-preservation. We will say and do anything to keep those actions and thoughts justifiable and okay in our own minds.

Who do you have in your life to keep you accountable?

How do you react when they do their job?

Kary Oberbrunner explains why a conformist's attitude runs us into trouble:

> We want to escape laws, rules, and dead faith. But by alienating ourselves from communities of faith, we end up conforming to culture rather than transforming it. We set our sights on cruise control and feast on everything the world offers, not once thinking about what's tolerable and what's toxic.[21]

---

[21] Oberbrunner, Kary. *The Fine Line: Re-envisioning the Gap Between Christ and Culture* (Grand Rapids, MI: Zondervan, 2008), p. 88.

I think we have all gone through this at some point. We have all made a decision without thinking about the consequences. Conformists usually end up trying to please other people before they look to please God. I think my friend with his bar buddies went through this. His actions became so clouded with what was acceptable in that social scene that the actions and words of Jesus were lost.

How can we teach one worldview when we are trying to live out our social lives in another? That is a huge obstacle when it comes to living the worldview of a conformist. Conformists attempt to fix the appearance of unhip Christians who are against everything from movie theatres to music, but oftentimes they go too far in trying to show what they are for rather than what they are against. Many times, when trying to find what they can be for, the boundaries or views of the church frustrate conformists. Church, in their minds, becomes a place of order and rules and has no room for anything on the hip radar. They start to remove themselves from the larger church body, attempting to find ways to incorporate society and God without looking like church.

The book of Hebrews gives a strong warning against this removal from church:

> So let's do it—full of belief, confident that we're presentable inside and out. Let's keep a firm grip on the promises that keep us going. He always keeps his word. Let's see how inventive we can be in encouraging love and helping out, not avoiding worshiping together as some do but

> spurring each other on, especially as we see the
> big Day approaching. (Hebrews 10:22–25)

How can these words help us move away from a conformist worldview?

It is found in these words: *"Let's see how inventive we can be in encouraging love and helping out, not avoiding worshiping together..."* The key becomes creativity. Conformists seem to lack the sense that the term "creative Christians" is not an oxymoron. In God's autobiography, the first chapter would be called *He Creates All*. That was his first objective, and even as God was creating he was extremely creative, changing things up, moving one step at a time. He went from light to life, creating everything in seven days.

Creativity is a process that takes work. Conformists lack this understanding of the creative process. To them, church and religion become stale, and instead of working and using their creative forces to help out their communities, they walk away. Instead of walking away from the church in search of culture, we should try to engage culture in our church communities through prayer and understanding, so that our communities can stay informed and relevant. When we lose faith in the creativity of our churches, we leave in search of something new, something *hip*, something other than church and its rules, but when we rely on the cultural messages to guide us we can easily fall into idolatrous ways. Paul was well aware of this possibility and took initiative to warn his communities about this danger.

> The thing that has me so upset is that I care
> about you so much—this is the passion of God
> burning inside me! I promised your hand in
> marriage to Christ, presented you as a pure
> virgin to her husband. And now I'm afraid that
> exactly as the Snake seduced Eve with his smooth
> patter, you are being lured away from the simple
> purity of your love for Christ. It seems that if
> someone shows up preaching quite another
> Jesus than we preached—different spirit,
> different message—you put up with him quite
> nicely. (2 Corinthians 11:2–4)

Do we allow the false promises of culture to lure us away from church?

Do we really think culture has more answers than Christ?

There is a great warning about a conformist heart in 2 Timothy: *"You're going to find that there will be times when people will have no stomach for solid teaching, but will fill up on spiritual junk food—catchy opinions that tickle their fancy. They'll turn their backs on truth and chase mirages"* (2 Timothy 4:3–4). It is important that we remember that being Christian does not mean we have to lack creativity, because the moment we think that we have no creative output we start searching for other areas to become involved.

Jonathan Dodson came up with six ways to engage culture and one of the first ways he wrote about was through prayer.

> When engaging culture prayerfully, we depend
> on the wisdom that comes from the Spirit who

> searches out all cultures, who can enable us to
> recognize and rejoice in what is true, beautiful,
> and good, and reject or redeem what is false,
> ugly, and immoral. As a result, engaging culture
> can become an act of communion with God.
> Relying on the wisdom of the Spirit will also
> mean careful investigation of cultural issues,
> being critical of our own biases while maintaining
> an open ear to the arguments of others.[22]

Conformists slowly begin to let the truth of God's word be replaced by the laissez-faire attitude of culture. Conformists lose their ability to go to God in silence and solitude because media becomes the guiding voice in their lives. The conformist camp, in search of freedom from rules and regulations, actually loses its creative force because it falls into the conformity of cultural norms and acceptance. They actually fall victim to the same rules they are running from. Lastly, they begin to tolerate instead of redeem.

Mad Men, a show that takes the audience into the lives of Madison Avenue ad men in the 1950s, portrays life through conformist eyes. The audience buys what they, the ad men, want us to buy. The consumer conforms his or her tastes in products to what people like Donald Draper tell us. In one scene, Rachel Menken, the owner of a high-class designer store, is in talks with Donald Draper about whether or not his agency should represent her store. She says, "Mr. Draper, I don't know what it is you really believe in, but I do know what it feels like to be out of place, to be

---

[22] Dodson, Jonathan. *Six Ways to Engage Culture*,
http://theresurgence.com/Six_Ways_to_Engage_Culture (accessed April 5, 2010).

disconnected, to see the whole world laid out in front of you the way other people live it. There is something about you that tells me you know it, too."[23] Conformists begin to see the world in that way. They want to live the way others are living because they do not want to disturb the peace of everyone around them. Everything begins to look acceptable and mouldable to fit God's truth, but the reality is that, more often than not, idolatry is the result of this worldview.

The third choice we have is to be transformists. In *A Journey Toward Relevance*, author Kary Oberbrunner addresses a very important question we need to ask ourselves if we want to be agents of transformation in the world: how do I hold onto my cross when I reach out into the darkness?

> Integrating our faith with our culture can only happen if we have a faith to integrate! When our faith is shallow, our hopes of transforming culture are shallow. In order for an agent to transform something, it has to be different from it. Many of us are no different than the culture to begin with.[24]

In order to fully establish ourselves as possible transformists, we have to center ourselves correctly. We must be holding onto our faith, but we also must be turning towards the world. The challenge with wanting to

---

[23] Weiner, Matthew. *Mad Men: Smoke in Your Eyes*, Television Series, directed by Alan Taylor, 2007.

[24] Oberbrunner, Kary. *The Journey Towards Relevence: Simple Steps for Transforming Your World* (Lake Mary, FL: Relevant Books, 2004), p. 127.

transform culture is that we need to gain a strong ability to listen to two voices at the same time.

Walt Mueller explains how and why it's important to gain the ability of double listening:

> ...the ability and resolve to listen to two voices at one time. He says that all Christians are called to "stand between the Word and the world, with consequent obligation to listen to both. We listen to the Word in order to discover evermore of the riches of Christ. And we listen to the world in order to discern which of Christ's riches are needed most and how to present them in their best light." With our understanding of the Word and the world as a foundation, we can contextualize the gospel by sharing it in a meaningful way to the emerging generations.[25]

I use this quote with everyone in my life who keeps talking about the "emerging church" as being evil. This covers a lot about what the emerging movement hoped to accomplish, but we'll come back to that a bit later.

The Apostle Paul is an amazing example of someone who has this ability of double listening. In Acts, Paul goes to Athens and sits in its community places—an ancient-day Starbucks, if you will—and engages the people in philosophy, religion, life, and their gods. He listens to everything they have to say both for and against God and still calmly talks to them about the unknown statue in their

---

[25] Mueller, Walt. *Engaging the Soul of Youth Culture: Bridging Teen Worldviews and Christian Truth* (Downer's Grove, IL: InterVarsity Press, 2006), p. 51.

midst.[26] Paul also has one of the best transformist stories imaginable. He went from being a Christian killer to a Christian defender and never took any credit for his transformation. In Philippians, Paul tells us about his transformed life.

> Steer clear of the barking dogs, those religious busybodies, all bark and no bite. All they're interested in is appearances—knife-happy circumcisers, I call them. The real believers are the ones the Spirit of God leads to work away at this ministry, filling the air with Christ's praise as we do it. We couldn't carry this off by our own efforts, and we know it—even though we can list what many might think are impressive credentials. You know my pedigree: a legitimate birth, circumcised on the eighth day; an Israelite from the elite tribe of Benjamin; a strict and devout adherent to God's law; a fiery defender of the purity of my religion, even to the point of persecuting Christians; a meticulous observer of everything set down in God's law Book.
>
> The very credentials these people are waving around as something special, I'm tearing up and throwing out with the trash—along with everything else I used to take credit for. And why? Because of Christ. Yes, all the things I once thought were so important are gone from my life. Compared to the high privilege of knowing Christ Jesus as my Master, firsthand, everything I once thought I had going for me is insignificant—

---

[26] Oberbrunner, Kary. *The Journey Towards Relevence: Simple Steps for Transforming Your World* (Lake Mary, FL: Relevant Books, 2004).

dog dung. I've dumped it all in the trash so that I could embrace Christ and be embraced by him. I didn't want some petty, inferior brand of righteousness that comes from keeping a list of rules when I could get the robust kind that comes from trusting Christ—God's righteousness.

I gave up all that inferior stuff so I could know Christ personally, experience his resurrection power, be a partner in his suffering, and go all the way with him to death itself. If there was any way to get in on the resurrection from the dead, I wanted to do it. (Philippians 3:2–11)

Living a transformist life is quite often the hardest of the three choices, because it takes a conscience choice to live it out. We have to decide to seek out the balance between knowledge of the word and the application of God's teaching. Too much of one leads to arrogance and too much of the other leads to a life rooted in the acceptance of every- one but Jesus. Like Paul, we need to make the choice between living like a separatist and acting like a conformist. Many times, we choose to live out a combination of these lives—separatist, conformist, and transformist—all at the same time. It comes back to the question about the line.

When you get together with other Christians, what do you watch? Do you watch nudity in films or on TV? Do you listen to angry or abusive music?

Becoming a true transformist requires us to make a true commitment to a biblical worldview with no ifs, ands, or buts. God requires us to sacrifice the entirety of our lives, a temple dedicated to him. Choosing that solitary life is an act of worship.

I have three ground rules which we should remember before we jump further into media:

- The Bible is very clear when it tells us to test everything. I believe that we have adopted a very different mindset these days, one that says, "Test nothing." We all read the same books, for one thing. Who hasn't read *Blue Like Jazz*, *The Shack*, or the books of Francis Chan? We all seem to read the same ten books. We don't test them, though. We don't test their validity against scripture. We just listen and believe. I hope you realize that I'm not saying these books go against the truth of the Scriptures; I'm saying that we need to test and ask ourselves the very same questions the authors ask in their books.
- I do not believe in the "us vs. them" mentality, or the idea of a separate "Christian" category when it comes to media.
- I have not arrived. I am not an expert in everything and I am on the same faith journey as you. I do what I do because I love young people and I love this discussion, simply because I didn't have this when I was growing up. I grew up in a world where we didn't talk

about challenging subjects when I asked about them.

It's a Sexy World Out There

I personally believe that there are two topics we as leaders and parents cannot avoid any longer. These are also the two talks I get booked for the most:

- My media.faith.culture talk, which includes a section on sex, and
- My dating.for.life talk.

Sex and dating—these are the two issues young people are dealing with most on a daily basis. So are we. The generation that our youth are growing up in has become vastly different than ours. If you're a late teen or in your early twenties, this goes for you, too. We live in a world where a Grade Twelve student looks at a Grade Eight student and says, "Who is this kid?"

That type of mentality used to take place between generations, but now they're saying "Who is this kid?" to people who are only a few years younger.

Think about the various ads out there that promote sex. We have cell phone ads with hands on butts, we have legs wrapped around liquor bottles, and we have billboards promoting websites like Ashley Madison. I once saw an Ashley Madison ad while driving through Toronto. They used to use the slogan, "When monogamy becomes monotony." Now they have ads with bylines like, "Life is short, have an affair" and "Who are you doing after the game?" This second slogan was intended for their Super Bowl XLIII campaign. It was denied by the NFL, to which Ashley Madison CEO Noel Biderman responded,

> I find the rejection to be ridiculous given that a huge percentage of the NFL's marketing content is for products like alcohol, which they sell in their stadiums, promote on their air and clearly have in the magazine... that's a product that literally kills tens of thousands of people each year. So if the NFL is worried about legislating behavior and regulating what their audience should be exposed to then it should start with a ban on all alcohol advertising and products sold, not AshleyMadison.com.[27]

Ashley Madison guarantees that when I get bored with my wife, I can log on and find another women to sleep with, a person who they guarantee will not turn around and tell my wife. It's an interesting world we live in, in which seeing this kind of thing becomes normal on our drive into work, or even while we watch a family event like the Super Bowl. The problem is that we, as the older generation, don't say anything about it.

These types of advertisements are starting to creep into the advertising and marketing of some of the biggest companies in the world. Microsoft launched an ad campaign where a student promoted Windows 7 by camping outside

[27] Pyle, Jon. "NFL Cracks Down on Cheating, But Not Like You Think," http://trueslant.com/jonpyle/2009/01/15/nfl-cracks-down-on-cheating-but-not-like-you-think/ (accessed January 28, 2011).

his dorm room while his roommate did some "private tutoring" with a female student.[28] Even though the premarital sex is only implied, the use of finger quotations and the sock on the doorknob is all the mind needs to connect the two.

When did sex become the most effective marketing tool to sell computers?

The ad talks about the connectivity and accessibility of Windows 7, which allows its users to watch TV shows anywhere, but is that really what you remember about the commercial? If we answered that question honestly, I think the answer would be the relationship between the roommate and the girl inside. The alarming factor is not that sex sells products, but that there's such an appalling silence from viewers over this type of marketing ploy.

According to the words of Martin Luther King, Jr., "In the end, we will remember not the words of our enemies, but the silence of our friends." What does our silence say about our culture? Does life really center around nothing but sex? Are we doing nothing to help those around us who struggle with sexual addiction and pornography? King also said, "Not only will we have to repent for the sins of the bad people, but we also will have to repent for the appalling silence of good people."

Ashley Madison promotes adultery. When we are silent about adultery becoming the norm in society, we begin to play a part in the normalization of adulterous behaviour.

---

[28] Microsoft. "Hallway—My Idea,"
http://www.youtube.com/watch?v=upXD78-owwQ (accessed March 20, 2011).

Mark Sayers, in his book *The Vertical Self*, has noted a shift that has occurred in culture. The word "sexy" no longer appeals to just sexual attraction; it now gives something—or someone, in most cases—value. "When people in our culture attempt to act out being sexy, they are just trying to act in a way that makes them desirable to others—not necessarily as a sexual partner, but often just as a person others find interesting and valuable."[29] When we started labeling sport plays and meals sexy, we started down a slippery slope into a world that places value and worth on an allure and not actions and heart.

How many songs can you think of that promote the allure of sexiness?

"Sexy" now determines value, desirability, and status of power... and that means sex will be everywhere. From billboards to music videos, the cultural object now has to have a sexy vibe just so it can sell in the store or crack the Hot 100. Culture has deemed that an object with sex appeal creates an aura of allure and creates a buzz of intrigue in the consumer.

We have all heard that sex brings power—we see that in the ads on TV and in the music video that played ten minutes ago—but the fact is this mentality has become such a social condition that sociologists have named this cultural phenomenon *performative sexuality*. "Sociologists have termed this phenomenon Performative Sexuality, noting that often this very public display of sexual power is often

---

[29] Sayers, Mark. *The Vertical Self* (Nashville, TN: Thomas Nelson, 2010), p. 60.

completely disconnected from one's personal sex life."[30] When you hear the term, you would think that it's talking about how you perform sexually with your spouse, but that could not be farther from the truth. Performative sexuality needs to be understood as an often very public display of sexual power that is completely disconnected from a person's sex life. "What is important is not what is going on in someone's real life, but how she, or he is putting on for the audience of their peers..."[31]

Sex is no longer private, passionate, or even special; sex is now a cultural phenomenon lived out in front of our peers for the whole world to see. Two questions need to be addressed for this cultural shift to be understood.

1) How did we get here?
2) How do we become agents of transformation?

The simple answer to the first question is the Internet and the technology boom that has occurred in your lifetime. The arrival of Google, Facebook, and video-sharing sites has changed how the world communicates and has made it easier to create silo lives (we will talk more about this later).

Think about it. When was the last time you said you would email someone? Or do you now tell them you will

---

[30] Sayers, Mark. "Beneath the Surface of 'Sexy': The Cautionary Tale of Brigitte Bardot," *Mark Sayers*, May 1, 2009, http://marksayers.wordpress.com/2009/05/01/beneath-the-surface-of-sexy-the-cautionary-tale-of-brigitte-bardot/ (accessed August 28, 2010).

[31] Sayers, Mark. *The Vertical Self* (Nashville, TN: Thomas Nelson, 2010), p. 62.

Facebook them? For myself, email was the shift away from phone calls and letters and was a shift based on time management. I could email ten people in the time it would take to call one person. Facebooking instead of emailing has been a shift based on ease and instantaneity.

Do you have a Facebook account?

I challenge every parent and leader to get a Facebook account. Why? Because that's where our kids are.

If you do have an account, how often do you check Facebook each day? Do you have Facebook on your phone?

Facebook is now a feature on most phones and some phones sold now are social-media-focused. Their sole goal is to make staying connected easier and more convenient in our hurried lives. This has become a change in culture. It has gone from telegrams to letters, phone calls to email, and now to Facebook.

How many of your friends are on Facebook? Or should I ask, how many of your friends are not on Facebook?

Facebook now has over 750 million users.[32] I used to be able to say that Facebook's population made it the fifth largest country in the world, but then something remarkable and unheard of happened. In eleven months, Facebook grew its user market by one hundred million users and has continued to grow at an alarming rate. Nothing in existence has ever grown that much in such a short time. *Time Magazine*, in May of 2010, released an article entitled *How Facebook Is Redefining Privacy*. The article was a study on the

---

[32] Facebook. "Statistics," https://www.facebook.com/press/info.php?statistics (accessed August 15, 2011).

privacy issues that have plagued the social media mogul, but it also established how popular Facebook has become.

> Facebook will officially log its 500 millionth active citizen. If the website were granted terra firma, it would be the world's third largest country by population, two-thirds bigger than the U.S. More than 1 in 4 people who browse the Internet not only have a Facebook account but have returned to the site within the past 30 days.[33]

Facebook has become such a cultural staple in households throughout Canada that more than half of us are users. Facebook has also become all about sharing. The same *Time* article explains our fascination with what we share.

> Facebook has changed our social DNA, making us more accustomed to openness. But the site is premised on a contradiction: Facebook is rich in intimate opportunities—you can celebrate your niece's first steps there and mourn the death of a close friend—but the company is making money because you are, on some level, broadcasting those moments online. The feelings you experience on Facebook are heartfelt; the data you're providing feeds a bottom line.[34]

Facebook is about making connections between what you share and what others share. On Facebook alone, there

---

[33] Ibid.
[34] Ibid.

are over nine hundred million things for people to interact with, whether it's info pages, groups, events, or community pages. On top of those, there are an additional thirty billion pieces of content, which includes news links, pictures, and blog notes.[35] It is all about emotionally connecting, but the question needs to be—what are we emotionally connecting to?

> The experience is designed to generate something Facebook calls the Aha! Moment. This is an observable emotional connection, gleaned by videotaping the expressions of test users navigating the site for the first time.[36]

The giants behind Facebook have come up with a number of Aha! Moments that a user needs to emotionally connect to in order to join. Which means that Facebook is created to garner emotional connections. They even play on your emotions if you try to leave the site and deactivate your account.

> And if you ever try to leave Facebook, you get what I like to call the Aha! Moment's nasty sibling, the Oh-no! Moment, when Facebook tries to guilt-trip you with pictures of your

---

[35] Facebook. *Statistics,*
https://www.facebook.com/press/info.php?statistics (accessed January 25, 2011)
[36] Fletcher, Dan. "How Facebook is Redefining Privacy," *Time Magazine*, May 20, 2010,
http://www.time.com/time/business/article/0,8599,1990582,00.html (accessed May 20, 2010).

friends who, the site warns, will 'miss you' if you
deactivate your account.[37]

The ease of emotional connection, and the way the
powers that be play on that connection, is what scares me
about how easily we share our experiences on the site. Do
we share too much without thinking about the
consequences?

Do we have anyone in our lives who can keep us
accountable for what we share? Is it a friend, sibling, or
family member? Are you "friends" with your students and
children on Facebook?

The problem with the internet explosion is that it will
never forget. I'm not saying that you should force your kids
to add you onto their Facebook account, but you might be
your child's best filter on what they do and do not post.

Do we really pay attention to those drunken photos
they posted last night? Do we challenge or discipline them
on their actions? If they don't care about you seeing the
photos, how will they feel about college administrators or
future employers seeing them?

The problem is that Google and the rest of the internet
do not forget. That what scares me, because many parents
miss this point. What kids post tonight will still be there
years from now for their children to see.

You may be saying, "Brett, that's years away and I don't
have to worry about their children being able to find
pictures of them online." Think about it this way: how
much better are your kids on the computer than you are?

[37] Ibid.

Do you go to your kids for advice with your computers? You should realize that your kids are that much better at surfing the web than you. That will continue into the next generation, their kids, and so on. In the next five, ten, and even fifteen years, those half-naked photos they took last night, or those photos with them drunk and passed out in front of a toilet, will not be that funny anymore.

Do you think they really want to explain that photo to their ten-year-old children someday? Challenging our kids on what they post today will stop some very embarrassing parental situations for them in the future.

I can look back online and find message boards that I posted on fourteen years ago while I was at university. The message boards are no longer active or even updated today, but thanks to Google what I posted years ago is still there, available to read, never to be forgotten.

Whenever someone adds me on Facebook, the first thing I will do is click "accept," and then I will check out their photos. Usually what I see breaks my heart. What breaks my heart is that the same girls who were just at one of my talks going on about justice, faith, and their relationship with God are in front of me once again. The difference is that what went from a great conversation about living out their faith at school or at home has been tainted because of the photo of her pushing her breasts together in front of a mirror for a photo on her Facebook page. The same eight-year-old girls who talk regularly about truth and justice are taking porn shots of themselves... and everyone thinks it's normal.

What are we doing about the message of self-worth when porn shots on Facebook are the norm?

The guys I meet are no different. I once met a particular boy from a Christian high school. He was, in fact, the student president of the Christian association at his school and he added me on Facebook after one of my talks. So like I said earlier, I went to see his pictures. The first picture on his profile page was him smoking pot from a bong. This is the president of a Christian association and he is sending the message that it is okay to smoke illegal drugs and post the photo along with it.

Do you not see where the message of living out our ancient faith with our modern day culture is lost?

It's not just speakers like me who check out your photos online and question your motives and heart. In an episode of *Dr. Phil*, Dr. Phil had on two girls who were confused as to why they did not get into college. They were confused because they were above average students with GPAs in the high 80s. But for some reason they did not get into university. The recruiters from the university were on the episode as well and very bluntly told the girls that the content they found online kept them from being accepted into the university of their choice.

Here is how the conversation broke down. The recruiters referred to pictures on their Facebook profiles that had them facedown, passed out in front of a toilet. What it looked like was a late night out that took a turn for the worse. The girls denied that the pictures were of them, to which the recruiters pointed out that it was one of their first pictures on Facebook. The point they were making was that the pictures painted a very bad image of the girls' lifestyle choices, which the university did not want to be associated with.

Universities and businesses are now aware of the social networking boom and have started taking advantage of the information that is available. A resume is no longer the piece of paper you send; it's become your top 10 results when they Google search your name. Like no other time in history, a future employer or school administration board can find out the very intimate details of your life. The fact is they will look at what the Internet says about you so that they can protect the integrity of their company or school.

Instead of them protecting their integrity, should we not be more worried about our integrity by what we post online?

Do you know how much it costs to have your history erased on the web? It costs ten thousand dollars to have your past erased, so that Google's claim of never forgetting becomes null and void.

The problem is that it's not your child who makes the payment. Do you have ten thousand dollars lying under your mattress that you're not planning to use for anything? What about the money you saved for their education? It will be you, the parent, who pays for their past to be erased. If your child lives like most young people out there who hide their internet self from their parents, they will have even more explaining to do.

Facebook has begun to change and shape the way we live. It allows for ease of communication and has provided an easy way to share our experiences with those closest to us. However, we have to be careful what and who we share our experiences with. Our lives are shaped by how others perceive us, and if we pervert the image we have for ourselves it is easy to become misjudged by others.

Here are some great resources to help you better understand social media and the trends behind it.

- *Mashable* (www.mashable.com)
- *The Twitter Guide Book* (www.mashable.com/guidebook/twitter/)
- *Social Media Examiner* (www.socialmediaexaminer.com)

The Pornification of Culture

Why has it become so easy to pervert our own lives? How has it become so easy for others to have a perverted view of each and every one of us? If you are over the age of twenty, you have witnessed what I like to call the "Pornification of Culture." Movies, music, and people have all eased up on what they consider too sexy or too racy. David Dark, the author of *The Sacredness of Questioning Everything*, challenges everyone to question how we have arrived at such a perverted state. His book begins at the point where we label others as hot, cool, handsome, and most often sexy.

> Reducing a person in this way is perversion, reducing them in the worst kind of way to an image for visual craving; it is a taking of the human form to market. A not-to-be-objectified

> beauty is reduced to the easy access of the
> voyeur whenever a person is primarily good for
> looking at.[38]

Do we want to be known as only being good to look at? Is that how we want to be remembered? That would quite possibly be the worst tombstone ever written: "Here lies Jon Smith. A father, a son, and a husband, but most importantly he was nice to look at." That would be horrible, but that is the message we hear every day in most of the music we listen to. Take an honest look at the lyrics of some of your favourite songs, or even pick a few off the radio. What do they tell us about each other and the opposite sex? What do the songs tell us to value or strive for?

I will say this: I believe that the pornification of culture is done. Why do I say that, even after I wrote that anyone over the age of twenty has witnessed its arrival? Simple. We witnessed the arrival, the takeover, and now we have reached the lowest point it can possible go. We now let kindergarten kids watch and listen to pornography, which I will dive into deeper later when we talk about the *Transformers* movies.

How many of your students and children have heard the songs we're about to cover? (See the chart just ahead.) Kids as young as two years old are experiencing the new, normal, pornified culture without question. Rihanna's *S&M* is one example of this culture shift.

---

[38] Dark, David. *The Sacredness of Questioning Everything* (Grand Rapids, MI: Zondervan, 2009), p. 76.

'Cause I may be bad, but I'm perfectly good at it.
Sex in the air, I don't care, I love the smell of it
Sticks and stones may break my bones
But chains and whips excite me

As you work through the Top Ten songs to follow, I think you will start to agree.

Let's try a little exercise. Here are the Top Ten songs from Billboard.com and the Canadian iTunes Store—at least, at the time this book was written. The next step in our exercise is to figure out what these songs are all about. What worldview do they promote? What values are lifted up? What do they make idols out of? Is anyone objectified or perverted in the lyrics? What does the song say is normal? All these questions will help us paint a picture of the world these songs invite us into.

SONG	ARTIST	WORLDVIEW
California Gurls	Katy Perry, feat. Snoop Dogg	Hot Girls + bikinis = sex on the beach.
OMG	Usher, feat. will.i.am	Lust is the ruling emotion.
Airplanes	B.O.B, feat. Hayley Williams	Fame does not equal happiness.
Billionaire	Travie McCoy, feat. Bruno Mars	Money = happiness.
Find Your Love	Drake	One-sided relationship.

SONG	ARTIST	WORLDVIEW
Your Love Is My Drug	Ke$ha	Love is like being high.
Alejandro	Lady Gaga	Sex.
Cooler Than Me	Mike Posner	What cool is.
Not Afraid	Eminem	Addictions.
Break Your Heart	Taio Cruz, feat. Ludacris	Emotions are cheap, so play with them.

That's the chart your students and children will have seen, so the next question is this: how do we engage them about the worldviews they are presented with every week on the Billboard Hot 100 list? Let's try this again, this time with a Top Ten list written a couple months after this book's first printing:

SONG	ARTIST	WORLDVIEW
Born This Way	Lady Gaga	Acceptance and inclusion, but missing the *truth*.
On the Floor	Jennifer Lopez, feat. Pitbull	Party hard without consequences.
S&M	Rihanna	All about sex.
E.T.	Katy Perry, feat. Kanye West	Act on physical attraction and sexual desires.

SONG	ARTIST	WORLDVIEW
Tonight	Enrique Iglesias	Tonight you're mine, tomorrow not so much.
Grenade	Bruno Mars	What would you sacrifice for love?
F**kin' Perfect	P!nk	Don't be defined by your flaws and self-image.
What the Hell	Avril Lavigne	Casual dating is fun.
I Need a Doctor	Dr. Dre, feat. Eminem & Skylar Grey	Mentorship and its role in relationships.
Hold It Against Me	Britney Spears	The power of seduction and persuasion

Your turn! Take ten minutes to go look up songs on www.billboard.com, www.mtv.com, or www.much-music.com. You can even look through your iTunes store.

SONG	ARTIST	WORLDVIEW

SONG	ARTIST	WORLDVIEW

Now, what do these songs tell you? Ask the same questions I asked about the songs that were on my list. What is normal? You might ask, "Why do I need to go and look up lyrics if you just did it for me?" Simple. This allows both of us to stay current and relevant in our knowledge of the media that is out there. The songs I wrote down were relevant when I wrote this book, but when you read this book those very songs are probably out of date. Music, like movies, are always changing. When we stop paying attention to what is new, we lose touch with reality.

Another great way to keep informed and relevant about the music and celebrities influencing the lives of our kids is to look up the Social 50 chart on Billboard.com.[39] The

[39] Billboard. *Social 50,*

Social 50 is a ranking of the top artists based upon their activity on social media websites like Twitter, MySpace, and Facebook. It's a great way to keep up to date regarding which artists are being talked about most frequently.

You might be thinking, *Isn't MySpace dead?* As a social networking site it is, but it continues to be one of the best online resources for up-and-coming artists to get their music out to the public. As an introduction to indie and local musical acts, MySpace continues to be one of the leading networking sites.

Many of these songs become normal in our everyday lives. We hear them in the car with our families, at school, at work, and at home. When we hear them, we sing along and think nothing of it. Have you ever taken the time to actually listen to the words our little brothers and sisters begin to sing?

One thing I need to note is the connection between the songs on the radio and the music videos we see on Much Music or MTV. For example, let's take Eminem's video for *Not Afraid*. The song has a positive message behind it when it comes to addictions and overcoming your addictions, but it is really hard to pick up on that message when you watch the video. In the song, Eminem talks about why he made the decision to clean himself up and move past his addictions.

> It was my decision to get clean. I did it for me.
> Admittedly, I probably did it subliminally for you

http://www.billboard.com/charts/social-50#/charts/social-50 (accessed January 25, 2011).

so I could come back a brand new me. You
helped see me through and don't even realize
what you did. Believe me you, I been through the
ringer, but they can do little to the middle finger.
I think I got a tear in my eye. I feel like the king of
my world. Haters can make like bees with no
stingers, and drop dead. No more beef flingers,
no more drama from now on. I promise to focus
solely on handling my responsibilities as a father,
so I solemnly swear to always treat this roof like
my daughters and raise it. You couldn't lift a
single shingle on it. Cause the way I feel, I'm
strong enough to go to the club or the corner
pub and lift the whole liquor counter up 'cause
I'm raising the bar. I shoot for the moon, but I'm
too busy gazing at stars, I feel amazing and...[40]

However, when you see the video for the first time the
message can get lost because the video looks like any other
Eminem video. The messages may be easy to look at on
paper, but the positive messages are easily lost in translation.
First, if we watch the video, what does it tell us?

Images of Eminem breaking through a brick wall
further carry the "recovery" theme, symbolizing
his battle against alcohol addiction and
prescription drugs. Other signs of the rapper's
desire for change: a promise to never let his fans
down again and "to focus solely on handling my
responsibilities as a father."[41]

[40] Eminem, Kobe, P!nk, Lil Wayne, and Rihanna. *Recovery*. (Santa Monica, CA: Aftermath Records, 2010).
[41] Afable, Melissa. "Culture and Media Institute," *Culture and Media Institute*, June 8, 2010,

Do you think a Grade Three student watching the video is able to understand all the hidden metaphors? Or are they just seeing Eminem acting and sounding like the old Eminem? *Not Afraid* proclaims the rapper's "decision to get clean"—but not without his customary cuss words. Eminem uses six variations of "f—" and three of "s—" in the four-minute song. The song also includes crude uses of the words "crap," "damn," "dick," and "middle finger."[42] Although Eminem's *Not Afraid* music video is chalk full of positive messages, when it comes to drug addiction there are many factors within the song and music video that can blur our lenses when it comes to understanding the worldview the song is portraying. The ability to question and look deep within the words and images of Eminem's video is difficult, especially when you are seeing and hearing them for the first time.

Let's take a quick look at a couple of the other songs on the list. First, let's start with Usher and *OMG*. Hopefully at this point you all know what OMG stands for, but just in case you don't, it stands for "Oh My God"—not "Oh My Gosh," as the song claims. Who actually says "gosh"? Or more accurately, who means "gosh" when they use OMG in a text?

Anyway, here is a male in his early thirties (born in 1978), singing a song about boobies and booty. "Honey got a booty like pow, pow, pow/honey got some boobies like

---

http://www.cultureandmediainstitute.org/articles/2010/20100608170031.aspx (accessed June 8, 2010).
[42] Ibid.

wow, oh wow."[43] Are you telling me an accomplished artist
and creative mind like Usher cannot come up with better
lyrics than this? The sad part is we have heard this from
Usher before, when he released *Here I Stand...* and it was
even done in two parts. "And now we're making love in
this club/And we're not gonna stop/Just because the people
in the club are watchin' us/Cause we don't give a damn
what they say."[44] All three songs are about the same thing—
a guy and a girl hooking up and having sex on the dance
floor while everybody is watching.

If I asked you what type of music you like, you would
probably not answer with, "Songs about sex." The reality is
that most of the songs getting radio play are about sex,
living large, and being idolatrous.

Ke$ha's songs *Tik Tok* and *Your Love Is My Drug* are all
about this worldview. I took my kids to school recently and
there was a young girl, maybe in Grade Two, walking along
with her ear buds in and singing loudly to Ke$ha's music.
Out of the mouth of a Grade Two student comes, "Wake
up in the mornin' feelin' like P-Diddy (Hey what's up
girl)/Grab ma glasses I'm out the door I'm gonna hit the
city (Let's go)/Before I leave brush ma teeth with a bottle of
Jack/'Cuz when I leave for the night I ain't comin' back."[45]

Here is a young girl singing about waking up hung-
over, drinking some Jack, and going back out to party. My
question is, does she even know what "Jack" refers to?

[43] Usher, Nicki Minaj, Ludacris, will.i.am, and T.I. *R V R*. (New York: LaFace, 2010).
[44] Usher, Young Jeezy, Will.i.am, Jay-Z, Beyoncé, and Lil Wayne. *Here I Stand*. (New York, NY: LaFace Records, 2008).
[45] Ke$ha. *Animal*. (United States: RCA/Jive, 2010).

Probably not, but it is normal because everybody listens and sings to songs without even questioning the influence they have in their lives. I have a concern when a Grade Two student is singing about getting drunk.

Ke$ha has been a pretty steady name on the top of the charts for over a year now. Her latest single to stay on the charts, *We R Who We R*, shows that her worldview has not changed:

> Got Jesus on my necklace
> Got that glitter on my eyes
> Stockings ripped all up the side
> Looking sick and sexyfied
> So let's go.[46]

It's yet another song by Ke$ha that promotes a lifestyle of partying, boys, and hookups. It isn't that we need to tell our young people what not to listen to, but we need to teach them to listen to the lyrics they sing so casually everyday.

Another artist making a huge wave on the charts is Bruno Mars. With hits like *Just the Way You Are* and *Grenade*, his voice will be quite recognizable for many teens out there. At first glance, *Grenade* seems to be about what Bruno Mars would be willing to do for love.

> I'd catch a grenade for ya...
> Throw my hand on a blade for ya...
> I'd jump in front of a train for ya...

---

[46] Ke$ha. *Animal + Cannibal.* New York, NY: RCA, 2010.

> I would die for ya baby;
> But you won't do the same.[47]

The questions we need to point out or make youth aware of are these: Why does he feel the need to sacrifice so much for her? What is he actually sacrificing? Is it obsession or love that he is feeling? What is the nature of their relationships?

The lyrics leave so many questions unanswered. The video ends with Bruno Mars actually throwing himself in front of a train because of the one-way relationship he is caught up in. This song provides a good correlation point between healthy dating relationships and empty obsession, or the pain of flirtatious advances which are meant as a joke but always leave one person emotional attached.

Just like Bruno Mars' look into the dangerous, addictive element of falling in love, Bella, in the *Twilight* series of books and films, falls into the same unrelenting search.

> About three things I was absolutely positive:
> First, Edward was a vampire. Second, there was a
> part of him—and I didn't know how dominant
> that part might be—that thirsted for my blood.
> And third, I was unconditionally and irrevocably
> in love with him.[48]

Bella, like many others, becomes delusional and obsessed with the one she loves, and it leads her to the conclusion that life isn't worth living without him. Bella

---

[47] Bruno Mars. *Grenade*. New York, NY: Elektra, 2010.
[48] Meyer, Stephenie. *Twilight* (New York, NY: Little, Brown Books for Young Readers, 2006), p. 195.

knows that the negatives outweigh the positives in their possible relationship, yet she finds her self-worth solely based in a relationship with Edward. This type of self-worth-defining relationship enters the lives of teenagers every day. Whether it comes from Bella Swan or Bruno Mars, the message is still the same: "My life is worth nothing apart from the other individual." It's a dangerous message, because this type of relationship should only be true of our relationship with Jesus.

Just the Way You Are is a great song with a clever and unique music video. It has Bruno Mars shaping his girlfriend out of the tape found within an old audio cassette. Each time he moulds her out of the tape, she tries to fix a portion of her image, but Bruno Mars continues to insist through his words and tabletop creation that she is, in fact, perfect the way she is. As the lyrics go, "Girl, you're amazing, just the way you are." The song gives the young men we teach and raise something to think about when it comes to the opposite sex.

Personally, I love this song and I bought it for my nine-year-old daughter's iPod. I love when I walk past her room and hear this song coming out of her speakers. These are the types of words I want her to hear over and over again—words that tell her she's worth something and that she is good enough just the way she is. The song teaches her that she is—and will be—loved for more than just her body, and that any boy worth her time will know this and tell her that every day of her life.

How are you speaking positively into the beauty of women in your life? It can be friends, girlfriends, or even sisters. What is media saying to uplift and shape positive self-image in the girls around us?

Check out some of the words spoken into the life of the woman in Bruno Mars' video:

- I'd never ask you to change.
- Cause you're amazing, just the way you are.
- Sad to think she don't see what I see.
- There's not a thing that I would change.
- If perfect is what you're searching for, then just stay the same.
- She's so beautiful, and I tell her everyday.
- Her lips, her lips, I could kiss them all day if she'd let me.

Did you catch that last line? "I could kiss them all day if she'd let me." This statement alone makes the song unique. It sends the message that intimacy and physical contact between two people needs to be consensual. The majority of the lines in the song are centered around positive reinforcement.

How many girls receive the opposite message from their significant others? Self-image is a huge stumbling block for many teens, and this song provides a positive example of how to speak into positive self-image.

Katy Perry released what was marketed as the song of the summer in *California Gurls*, which features Snoop Dogg. It has also been mentioned as a possible anthem for the state of California in the same way that Frank Sinatra's *New York,*

New York—or more recently, Jay-Z's *Empire State of Mind*—
was an anthem for New York. There is one big difference,
however, that sets *California Gurls* apart. It does not look at
the greatness of California; instead it focuses on a minority.
The song is all about hot girls and their stereotypes.

How would you feel if you were a young girl living in
California struggling with your identity and beauty and you
hear this song everywhere? Every girl in California who has
any value whatsoever must be "unforgettable/Daisy Dukes,
bikinis on top/Sun-kissed skin, so hot will melt your
Popsicle."[49] Apologies to any fair-skinned young women in
California, or any girl with modesty who does not stroll
around in short shorts all day... according to Katy Perry,
your value is diminished. What kind of world do we live in
when our girls are starving themselves to look a certain way
because the media tells them they have to be a beach babe
in order to have any value? Think of how many girls in
your youth groups are struggling in some way with their
self-image, and yet we wonder how these feelings get
hooked so deep in their lives.

One way you might want to look at the issue of self-
esteem and the value of women is to watch some
MuchMusic or MTV and write down the various messages
that come through. One example would be the videos for
Katy Perry's *California Gurls* and *Teenage Dream*, and
compare them to the message in Bruno Mars' *Just the Way
You Are*.

Both artists speak into the lives of young women; one
for the negative and one for the positive. While Katy

---

[49] Perry, Katy and Snoop Dogg. *Teenage Dream*. (New York, NY: Capitol, 2010).

focuses on partying, casual sex without consequences, and
how "normal" girls should look, Bruno Mars tells the
young woman in the video that she's perfect just the way
she is. Even when she doesn't like her eyes or her smile,
they are perfect to him because her identity and worth goes
much deeper than her surface features.

Try these kinds of exercises with the youth around you
so that you can gain a better understanding into the
messages they are actually hearing. You might be surprised
by what they hear and pull out of certain songs.

Katy Perry's latest songs, *Firework* and *E.T.*, just like the
majority of her new album, lead her listeners into a less than
ideal worldview. As you listen to the album, try the same
exercise: ask the girls in your group, or your children at
home, to write out the worldviews of each song. Also, pick
out some lyrics that could be either positive or negative and
allow the girls to come to some conclusions about what
type of music they like to listen to everyday.

At one point in her life, Katy Perry went by the name
Katy Hudson and released a self-titled album under the
music label Red Hill. My daughter Zoe still listens to it and
even now Katy Perry regularly comments on her religious
beliefs and upbringing. In an interview in Blender
magazine, first published in October 2008, she spoke about
her Jesus tattoo on her wrist. "I see it every time I'm
playing guitar. It's looking back up at me. That's where I
come from, and probably where I'm going back to."[50]

---

[50] Perry, Katy. "Culture Clips," *Focus on the Family's Plugged In Online*,
October 13, 2008,
http://www.pluggedin.com/cultureclips/2008/october132008.aspx (accessed
August 10, 2010).

In the August 19, 2010 issue of *Rolling Stone*, Katy Perry says very public dispute with Lady Gaga over the Alejandro video stems from her religious background.

> "I wrote that tweet because of a combination of things," says Perry. "I am sensitive to Russell taking the Lord's name in vain and to Lady Gaga putting a rosary in her mouth. I think when you put sex and spirituality in the same bottle and shake it up, bad things happen. Yes, I said I kissed a girl. But I did not say I kissed a girl while f—ing a crucifix."[51]

Although she is very blunt about what makes her uncomfortable when it comes to sexuality and religion, she is making many Christian girls who love her music feel that exact same way. The tweet she referred to was "Using blasphemy as entertainment is as cheap as a comedian telling a fart joke."[52] If we are going to talk about Katy Perry and the religious journey she is on, it means nothing if we do not take things one step further. There is no sense talking about her coming back to a religion she feels confused about if we are not willing to pray for her and her journey. It is about time that we start praying for the lives of the very artists we are so quick to judge.

I have gone into churches that have been playing Lady Gaga:

---

[51] Grigoriadis, Vanessa. "Sex, God and Katy Perry," *Rolling Stone*, August 2010, p. 47.
[52] Ibid.

Hold me and love me
Just want to touch you for a minute
Baby three seconds is enough for my heart to
     quit
Let's have some fun
This beat is sick
I wanna take a ride on your disco stick
Don't think too much just thrust that stick
I wanna take a ride on your disco stick.[53]

In a world where we are called to flee sexual immorality of any kind, this should not be played during our youth times. It goes against the very worldview we are called to live.

Have you seen the video for the song *Alejandro*? I will save you the time and energy; it is Lady Gaga in her bra and underwear walking around. At the end, she takes her top off and nine or ten guys fall on top of her.

Yes, sex sells, but it will only take you so far. Lady Gaga is a phenomenal artist, so why does she have to rely on sex to sell albums? There are many artists out there who have commented on how talented she is. T.I. recently told MTV that her talent is shown through her ability to work with a wide range of artists that span numerous genres. "She is a phenomenal talent, and I think that talent transcends through all genres, all races, all religions, all countries."[54]

---

[53] Lady Gaga, Colby O'Donis, Space Cowboy, and Flo Rida. *The Fame.* (Santa Monica, CA: Interscope Records, 2008).
[54] Ziegbe, Mawuse, and Kelly Marino. "MTV News," *MTV*, June 28, 2010, http://www.mtv.com/news/articles/1642544/20100628/t_i_.jhtml (accessed August 5, 2010).

He continued in the same interview to point out why she has become so successful through her immense talent. "I believe that that's one thing that everybody can agree on. If you like a song and I like a song, then we going to both dance and all that here together... I think that that's what she's the best example of."[55]

Lady Gaga's *Born This Way* speaks of the need for acceptance, but it also questions some very strong biblical principles.

> Yes, God has made us just the way He wanted to, instilling in us tremendous value and worth. The Scriptures are clear on that. But we are sinful and polluted beings who need to exercise Biblical discernment in our assessments of ourselves, our natures, what we believe, and how we live. Without a deep and sobering understanding of our own sin, we can never fully understand or appreciate the grace we received at the cross. The song puts forth and promotes a way of thinking about, looking at, and living life that's been increasingly embraced in our culture. We are who we are... but we need to be who we've been called to be. Lady Gaga is making some powerful statements about the nature of God, the nature of humanity, the nature of sin, and how to live life. The whole world is watching, listening, and believing.[56]

---

[55] Ibid.

[56] Mueller, Walt. *Lady Gaga... Born This Way... The Voice of a Generation?* http://learningmylines.blogspot.com/2011/02/lady-gaga-born-this-way-voice-of.html (accessed February 2, 2011).

The questions of sexuality, individuality, and acceptance in *Born This Way* are the questions of this generation.

> We need to address the feelings at the core of this message. If this is the song for a new generation, why is it coming as such a surprise? It leads us to ask one simple question, are we creating an atmosphere of acceptance? In creating that atmosphere, how are we reacting to those broken relationships found within our biblical worldviews?[57]

Lady Gaga's immense popularity allows her to raise issues, but it is up to us to point our youth towards the correct worldview.

You can even look at the fact that Lady Gaga's talent was showcased on the very successful first season of *Glee*. She has also worked with the likes of Beyonce and Elton John. Her talent is unmistakable, but again it comes down to how the talent is interpreted. Is her talent clouded by her questionable sexual innuendoes and suggestive lyrics, or does it shine through in her musical and vocal talent? The only way to answer those questions is to question the worldviews of the songs and videos that artists put out.

Is sex all we are really looking for when it comes to the music we listen to?

I will take the most simplistic sexual line ever. Rihanna is one of the hottest artists on the planet and, in case you

[57] Clarke, Adam B.R. "Have You Gone 'Gaga' for Gaga?" *The Emerging Network* www.theemergingnetwork.com/The_Emerging_Network/Narrative/Enteries/ 2011/2/15_Have_you_Gone_Gaga_for_Gaga.html (accessed February 15, 2011).

don't remember, her boyfriend Chris Brown a couple of years ago abused her. What we need to look at is that 47% of teenagers believe she deserved it.[58] Almost half of your friends, schoolmates, and family think she deserved to be abused by her boyfriend. Both individuals are responsible for the events that occurred that evening. However, we need to understand that violence is a selective response. We can blame all kinds of factors when it comes to our actions, but the actions we carry out and act upon are controllable. We don't punch a cop when we get a ticket, we don't bite a teacher for a failing grade, and we do not scratch at our pastor's flesh when he challenges us on our words and actions.

Some helpful music resources are:

- www.pluggedin.com
- www.itunes.com
- Rolling Stone Magazine (www.rollingstone.com)
- Relevant Magazine (www.relevantmagazine.com)
- Billboard Magazine (www.billboard.com)
- MTV News app
- VEVO HD app, or the VEVO music channel on YouTube

---

[58] Hoffman, Jan. "Teenage Girls Stand by Their Man," *The New York Times*, March 18, 2009, http://www.nytimes.com/2009/03/19/fashion/19brown.html?_r=2&pa (accessed June 5, 2010).

- www.CPYU.org
- www.thesource4ym.com

Guys, I want you to pay attention to this: your size alone can be intimidating enough. I am a big guy and my size alone can be intimidating when I walk into a room. If I wanted to, I could use my size to my advantage, but I don't. Intimidation is just as selective as striking out against someone.

There is no reason, ever, for which a woman deserves to be hit or abused in any way. Learn that and live by that every day.

Ladies, you also have to realize that you have the same responsibility to the men in your life. I hear stories of guys who are abused by their girlfriends, and that isn't acceptable, either. Abuse is abuse, no matter whether it is happening to a guy or a girl. Let that sink in a little bit. There is nothing you could ever do to deserve being touched inappropriately by any guy or girl.

"Brett, what if she cheated?"

I was actually asked that once. My response is simple: "Then you break up with her. You don't hit her."

The sexual reference in her song goes like this: "I want to see how you move it... You wanna come get me outta my dress?"[59] Is this acceptable? Is this normal? How about for a Grade Four student? How about my daughter? She is in Grade Three. No one would think it is okay for my

---

[59] Rihanna, Jay-Z, and Ne-Yo. *Good Girl Gone Bad*. (New York: Island Def Jam, 2007).

daughter to sing a line like that, but for us it is okay because we justify that it is just a song and the words are harmless.

From my fourteen years of traveling and speaking to both parents and young people (both Christian and otherwise), I have found that there's no real restrictions to the type of media that comes into their homes.

Recently, I spoke to a group of about a thousand students and asked them how many of them had any kind of filter on the content they accessed on their home computers. You know how many students raised their hands? One. One kid raised his hand. *One.* That's absolutely crazy.

Why don't we have filters on our family computers? Many of our students are allowed to listen, watch, and download with little to no influence from anyone in the home.

As a leader, how often do we use this excuse to allow anything into our lives just so that we can be relevant? We need to be able to talk to our kids about it, right? At some point, though, that excuse doesn't cut it. I understand that we need to see certain things for ourselves in order to understand culture, but at what point does this lack of a filter ruin our own family lives? God tells us to flee sexual immorality, but instead of fleeing are we just walking slowly away while peeking over our shoulder?

What songs do we as leaders have on our iPods that we have told youth not to have? Is there any difference in them listening to it and seeing it on our iPods? Does that then, in their eyes, justify them listening to those songs, making us hypocrites?

As leaders, we do have an added responsibility towards the music we promote and play at our youth events. I once walked into a church where the pastor's wife was playing Lil Wayne's *Lollipop* on her iPod, and she tried to convince me that it was a good song.

Lil Wayne is a little removed from the charts, but the idea is still the same. What are we playing as entrance/exit music for our gatherings? What messages are we sending without even realizing it? The interesting part for me is looking at what we do and don't know. That pastor's wife didn't know the sexual reference behind the song and actually thought the song was about lollipops, not strippers spinning around their poles. It's about time that we actually learned the cultural references to the songs that are unconsciously entering our students' worldviews.

Text Talking

This idea of cultural understanding goes far beyond music and media, though. I was talking to another pastor's wife—trust me, I'm not picking on pastors' wives—and she ended one of her sentences with a chuckle and the expression "WTF." As youth workers, we've heard it all, read it all, but nothing in the world could have prepared me for this interaction.

"Excuse me...?"

This was all I could really get out before she repeated it, "WTF," almost sheepishly. I could almost hear the questions running wild in her mind.

"Do you know what that means?" I asked. "It means what the f—."

I watched that woman die on the inside. She said that she had heard her daughter use it. She had used it in front of women's groups, and indeed all over. Our first rule should be not to use text speak anywhere. I don't know too many people who use LOL after a sentence. We just don't do that.

Have you ever been on your youth's Facebook page? We now have some LOL extrapolations—like LMFAO ("laughing my f—ing a— off"). Is that really necessary? It's about time we began to look at what kind of language has become normal. The majority of people don't even know what it means. There's a quote in the movie *Definitely, Maybe* where Kevin Kline's character reads from his latest book:

> The most endangered species in our nation isn't a big woodpecker, or a fresh water fish, it is the tongue in our heads. Listen to the... language of today. The average vocabulary is a third of what it was a hundred years ago. Words fall out of our mouths and die at our feet. The landscape of vocabulary is being hacked down and grubbed up by the dribble of pop culture. Poisoned by lazy obscenities... [60]

Just like Kevin Kline's rant, vocabulary has changed with the texting boom. LOL, WTF, and the OMGs of language have taken over. If you're not sure what's being

---

[60] *Definitely, Maybe*. Directed by Adam Brooks, Universal (2008).

texted to you by your youth, or do not even know what they are saying when they drop acronyms, you need to do some more research. Try a website like www.texted.ca or www.netlingo.com and read through their acronictionary for some extra guidance. As leaders, the rule of thumb should be not to say anything if you don't know what it means. Try deciphering some of these:

WORD	MEANING	WORD	MEANING
KOTL		BIO	
AYDY		BBS	
CUL8R		CYE	
DL		MYO	
NE1		RYS	
SLAP		TTYL	
TWSS		BAG	
CD9		CU46	
PAL		PRON	
SOE		UG2BK	

(Key available on page 304.)

The Reality of Gaming

The pornification of culture has penetrated much deeper than the lyrics of our favourite songs. Video games have also been introduced which follow the adage that sex outsells everything. Gaming today is bigger than music, and perhaps even bigger than television, but I can actually remember a time without video games. That's right—*no video games!*

Then one day there was *Pong*—the game with two white rectangles and one circle. That was my video game life, and then everything changed. I could turn that little white ball green, and at that moment I told my buddy that I had arrived, because I could now change the colour of the ball. What else could I possibly want?

Well, we also had a game called *Skeet Shooter*. Not too far from *Pong* in terms of graphics, but there was one big difference—full colour. I can still remember a conversation I had with a girl about the relevance of this game and the difference between my generation and her generation.

"Notice how he only had one arm?" I asked.

She said, "You're wrong. That's his gun."

"Well, honey, then he has no arms."

We didn't care about the arms, because we had video games. Would you be satisfied if all you had was *Pong* or *Skeet Shooter*? We didn't even care about change of scenery. *Pole Position* had mountains that never changed. You could drive in a circle and they would always look exactly the same.

Do you honestly think that would sell now?

Honestly?

I would also play games like *Asteroids*, *Pac Man*, *Ms. Pac Man*, and of course *Donkey Kong*. This was the beginning of character development within videogames.

> Pac Man... had a life. He had a wife. He had children... It was not narrative... but it was giving life to these characters... In short, someone wanted something, he would go through a lot to get it, and his attempts would take place within chapters and levels. By taking that conceit and bottlenecking it with the complications of "story," the modern video-game narrative was born.[61]

That's what allows games like *Donkey Kong* to be able to make comebacks, only with a little rebranding, as my six-year-old son reminds me every time I say "*Donkey Kong.*"

"DK, Dad! It's DK!"

Without a doubt, the gaming world has changed. Now we can buy all these old games together on one console. It's called the Arcade Collection.

Video games have changed dramatically since the days of *Pong* and *Donkey Kong*. Video games are now the norm in households instead of the exception. Video games are now online, handheld, and even wireless. Arcades are a thing of the past because everyone has access to some sort of video game every day in North America. Gaming is bigger than TV, bigger than movies, music, and the reality is that what I knew as gaming isn't gaming anymore. It has changed dramatically over the years.

---

[61] Bissell, Tom. *Extra Lives: Why Video Games Matter* (New York, NY: Pantheon Books, 2010), p. 17.

However, we're the greatest gaming generation. The 20–40 age range is considered to be the generation with the most gamers. That's because those people have money and time. The high school age range has the next largest, followed by junior high. The best way for you to get an idea which games your youth are playing is simply to ask.

The reality of gaming can be found in the enormous sales of the video game franchise *Grand Theft Auto*. The franchise has sold almost 90 million copies worldwide, with just about half of those sales coming from North America.[62] The amount of units sold places it well within the top ten video game franchises of all time. I tell you this because unlike some of the other franchises on that list, the reality and worldview promoted by *Grand Theft Auto* is not biblical. The reality of the game is that I can drive around, pick up a prostitute, have sex with her in the car while she screams out the F-word, and then kill her when I am done.

> While the passerby and pedestrians you slay out of mission will occasionally drop money, it would be hard to argue that the game rewards you for indiscriminate slaughter. People never drop that much money, for one, and the best way to attract the attention of the police, and begin a hair-raising transborough chase, is to hurt an innocent person. As for the infamous cultural trope that in GTA you can hire a prostitute, pay her, kill her, and take her money, this is also true. But you do not have to do this. The game certainly does not

[62] VG Chartz, "Software Totals," *VG Chartz*, http://www.vgchartz.com/worldtotals.php?name=Grand%20Theft%20Auto (accessed June 10, 2010).

> ask you to do this. Indeed, after being serviced
> by a prostitute, Niko will often say something
> like, "Strange. All that effort to feel this empty."
> Outside of the inarguably violent missions, it is
> not what GTA IV asks you to do that is so morally
> alarming. It is what it allows you to do.[63]

I hope you caught those last two lines: "It is not what GTA IV asks you to do that is so morally alarming. It is what it allows you to do." Although GTA asks you to do some pretty unspeakable actions, some of the content needs to be acted upon in order to experience it in gameplay. That means it isn't the game placing the content in front of our youth, it is our youth thinking up that content and how to make it happen within gameplay. Our kids are now controlling morality within a game. They can argue, manipulate, and justify immoral acts within a gaming structure for entertainment value.

Now, ask the youth around you what they play.

Video Game	Video Game

---

[63] Bissell, Tom. *Extra Lives: Why Video Games Matter* (New York, NY: Pantheon Books, 2010), p. 173.

Video Game	Video Game

Also ask them questions like these:

- What values does the game represent?
- How does the game depict women/men?
- Do you control the moral decisions of the character you play?
- What decisions do you justify as you play?
- How do you justify those decisions?
- What worldview is being played out on the screen?

Some video games, like *Star Wars: Knights of the Old Republic* and *Mass Effect*, allow choice to dictate how your character evolves, with morality being one of the key ingredients to character growth.

> Here, as in later Mass Effect, almost every conversation and encounter initiated by the gamer can lead to multiple and often drastically different outcomes, some of which bring you in line with the Force, some of which tempt you down the path of the dark side of the Force. The game changes—as does your character's appearance—depending on where he or she falls along a spectrum of in-game morality.[64]

The danger in something like this is that players have the ability to create for themselves a moral universe to guide their lives outside of gameplay. Circumstantial decisions made in gameplay can carry over into the real world, affecting a person's worldview. At this point, morality and worldview become, like we talked about earlier, all about where you draw your line. Biblical worldviews take a back seat to perceived morality, which is chosen for entertainment value instead of sustaining value.

Another alarming feature of the new war-based video games is the reality of the games' setting. Both *Medal of Honor* and *Call of Duty* have allowed the player to put themselves in some very questionable shoes.

> Gunning down Americans in video games as an enemy force is not new. Previous installments of the Electronic Arts-produced game were set

---

[64] Ibid., p. 106.

during World War II and allow gamers to kill
Allies playing Axis soldiers. MoH rival "Call of
Duty" allowed terrorist-style avatars to kill
Americans, but kept the peace by dubbing
evildoers "OpFor," short for opposition forces.
Leaving World War II behind for Helmand
Valley or gritty Kabul, MoH's online multiplayer
mode pits elite "Tier 1 Operators" against—
naming names—Taliban fighters.[65]

This role reversal feature gives off some very serious
mixed messages. What does this feature tell young people
about the state of the world today? Do they understand the
reality of what is happening in Afghanistan and other war-
torn countries if they can battle it out fictitiously everyday?

"Right now, we're going into a really, really bad
time in Afghanistan," Meredith said. "This game is
going to be released in October so families who
are going to be burying their children are going
to be seeing this."
Amanda Taggart, EA's senior public relations
manager, told AOL News on Aug. 13 that MoH is
a game like any other.
"Most of us have been doing this since we
were 7—if someone's the cop, someone's gotta
be the robber, someone's gotta be the pirate
and someone's gotta be the alien," Taggart said.
"In 'Medal of Honor' multiplayer, someone's
gotta be the Taliban."[66]

---

[65] Gould, Joe. "Play-as-Taliban option in game causes stir,"
http://www.armytimes.com/news/2010/08/army-play-as-taliban-video-game-
093010w (accessed April 15, 2011).
[66] Ibid.

For the record, Meredith's son lost his life in Afghanistan and now she has to watch her reality being played out daily in a videogame. The same can be said for all the parents and families who watch over the Highway of Heroes in Ontario as our fallen soldiers return home.

Role reversal in video games is not as simple as cops and robbers; it's a heartbreaking reminder of the reality of war for many families.

> "Their argument is generally if you don't want to play it, don't buy it, but my son didn't get to start over. When he was killed, his life was over, and I have to deal with that every day," [Meredith] said.[67]

The lines between fiction and reality are becoming less and less clear. Especially when our students can now play out a present-day war while a family suffers through the tragedy of losing their child in the same war.

One night I was scheduled to speak to a youth group and I walked into the building to find the group and the youth pastor playing video games on a big screen. They were playing one of the *Grand Theft Auto* titles—more specifically, the youth pastor was playing it. When I walked in, the game was on a scene where the characters on-screen were engaged in sexual acts. The youth pastor stopped playing to come over to meet me and asked what I was going to be speaking on that night. I paused in confusion and said, "You."

---

[67] Ibid.

What is that?!

Is that really what is normal today?

The reality of culture is that we are now giving games like *Grand Theft Auto* to kindergarten students because it is a normal game for young kids in lower grades. When you go to Wal-Mart and buy a game that says nudity right on the cover, you need to ask yourself what you're doing.

What is the difference between buying that game and renting porn?

However, it wasn't these online video games that caused the first stir in the pornification of video games. One of the first games was *Custer's Revenge*, a game in 1982 that had such objectionable content that Atari ultimately sued the game's developer, Mystique, in an effort to publicly distance the Atari console from the game's negative media attention. The game was developed to be a dramatic historical recreation of the battle of Little Big Horn, slightly rewritten to appeal to growing adult fantasies of the time. Instead of being killed by the savage, godless Sioux and Cheyenne Indians, Custer walks through arrow fire to engage a woman tied to a cactus.

MMO (massively multiplayer online) have taken off and provide players with new online lives and experiences. Websites like www.raptr.com allow users to log in and track the amount of hours they spend playing MMOs and their other favourite games through an Internet connection. It also allows you to see how many hours other online users are spending playing these games. If you play these titles, try keeping track of how long you are playing them over a one-week span. Some of the most popular titles are:

MMO TITLE	AVG. HOURS PLAYED (JANUARY–FEBRUARY, 2011)
Call of Duty 2: Black Ops	2,625,335
World of Warcraft	1,693,540
CityVille	792,632
Halo: Reach	742,295
Assassin's Creed: Brotherhood	444,200
Call of Duty: Modern Warfare 2	327,778
Fallout: New Vegas	285,315

MMO TITLE	HOURS PLAYED DURING ONE WEEK

MMO TITLE	HOURS PLAYED DURING ONE WEEK

The key to understanding the MMO fad is found in the addictive component of these games, especially the MMOs like *World of Warcraft*, *Star Craft*, and even *FarmVille*. Originally *World of Warcraft* started with sixty levels, but then an expansion came out with another ten, and then they released *another* ten levels. Now this trend is even more evident in the games on Facebook—the problem is that these games do not finish. Every time you get to the end of *World of Warcraft*, they add a new level to download.

Another example of this is the new smash hit *LittleBigPlanet* and the sequel, *LittleBigPlanet 2*. In a new commercial for *LittleBigPlanet 2*, the audience is made aware of the infinite possibilities of the gameplay. The ability to create and share created worlds online with friends, and with downloadable new content from Sony gameplay, could quite easily become an addiction. *LittleBigPlanet*, *Oblivion*, and in some ways *World of Warcraft* represent sandbox-type gaming.

> ...open world or sandbox or free-roaming game... sensation of being inside a large and disinterestedly functioning world, a main story line that can be abandoned for subordinate story lines (or for no purpose at all), large numbers of supporting characters with whom meaningful interactions is possible, and the

ability to customize (or pimp, in the parlance of
our time) the game's player-controlled central
character.[68]

For someone like me with a very addictive personality,
this type of game is dangerous, because I have to finish a
game. These sandbox-type games give the gamer freedom
to explore without the pressure of time.

> So: two hundred hours playing Oblivion? How is
> that even possible?... In the world of Oblivion
> you can also pick flowers, explore caves, dive for
> treasure, buy houses, bet on gladiatorial arena
> fights, hunt bear, and read books. Oblivion is less
> a game than a world that best rewards full
> citizenship, and for a while I lived there and
> claimed it... What this means is that the first
> several hours I spent inside Fallout 3 were, in
> essence, optional. Even for an open-world game,
> this suggests an awesome range of narrative
> variability.[69]

As you can see, this free range of gameplay strongly
hinders one's ability to finish. I have dealt with students as
young as Grade Three on video game addiction. At some
point, parents need to take responsibility and simply turn off
the game. This is a serious problem. It's not unusual for
youth to sit down and play for at least three hours straight
without breaks.

---

[68] Bissell, Tom. *Extra Lives: Why Video Games Matter* (New York, NY: Pantheon
Books, 2010), p. 4.
[69] Ibid., p. 5, 7.

IMVU is a chat program. In it, you can climb on my lap and give me a virtual lap dance as we chat online. The world has changed dramatically.

Another attraction to these games is the ability to create and live "siloed" lives. In other words, our youth can create multiple forms of themselves—whether for school, gameplay, or on Facebook. They create personas that they tell us about, and others for friends. That allows them to have a clean profile with acceptable photos on one, and another where they can post their party photos and say their WTFs.

Need some video game resources? Try these:

- www.raptr.com
- *Extra Lives,* by Tom Bissell (New York, NY: Pantheon Books, 2010)
- PlayStation Magazine
- *Flickering Pixels*, by Shane Hipps (Grand Rapids, MI: Zondervan, 2009)
- www.vgchartz.com
- www.whattheyplay.com

The Problem with Texting

Texting is another huge problem. To be honest, I love it, but my problem is not with texting. The problem I address today is an emerging trend in culture centering on sex and texting—we call it "sexting." First off, it's an extremely dumb name. It is not just an issue of two people writing sexual messages back and forth, though. The problem I run into is the young woman who takes a half-naked picture of herself and emails it to her boyfriend. The boyfriend is an idiot and then sends it to his friends. A recent study says that one-fifth of all forwarded pictures are sent beyond the initial receiver, which means that any private picture, no matter what the guy says, is usually sent to his friends and beyond. I then get calls asking, "Brett, what do I do? It's all over my school!"

I've worked with families that have had to deal with their daughter sending a topless photo of herself to her boyfriend. I've seen how little the police do in addressing the problem. One girl I knew got off with a slap on the wrist and a basic warning not to do it again, but the reality is that the photo is still public to the students at her school. For that girl, that photo is an everyday reality. My only suggestion would be for the family to move to a new town. That's the only way I can think of to have that photo lose its power over that girl's future.

It doesn't matter whether the picture was meant to be private of not. Once it gets shared, the law is the solution. The solution is to charge the girl with creating child pornography. I deal with young Christian girls in Grade Seven who are charged and are now considered registered sex offenders. The boy is charged with distributing child pornography and is now a registered sex offender as well. And so are any of their friends who have the photo on their phone.

Think about that for a second. One mistake and your life is turned upside down because of one simple picture.

Role models today are just awesome—you cannot hear me say this right now, but know that there is a strong sarcastic tone in my voice. Rihanna has been quoted as saying, "If you don't send your boyfriend naked pictures, then I feel bad for him..."[70] *Really?* Her influence is not just with the teens she influences, but preteens as well. It is quite possible that your younger sisters are hearing that they should send naked photos to the boys they have a crush on. Rihanna has actually admitted to feeling humiliated. "I just felt like my whole privacy was taken before that, and then, when that came out, I thought, 'Oh great, so now there's nothing they don't know about me and my private life.'"[71]

It sure doesn't sound like it was a good decision to me. We need to start speaking to our junior high students more about content like this. The time between Grades Six and Eight are so important. If we teach them early, we stop the Band-Aid ministry model for those in high school and young adults. Yes, they will squirm, but talk about sex with them. They already hear it at school, on their iPods, and on the TV, so address the issue with them from a biblical standpoint. Tell them you'll use words like masturbation and allow them to have weird looks on their faces. Be uncomfortable today so that you don't have to deal with problems later.

---

[70] Collins, Leah. "Rehanna's Relationship Advice," *Vancouver Sun*, November 27, 2009,
http://www.vancouversun.com/entertainment/Rihanna+relationship+advice+send+your+boyfriend+naked+pictures+then+feel/2276859/story.html (accessed August 2010, 2010).
[71] Ibid.

This will help to eliminate some of the hurt down the road. I have ministry friends who go through a healthy relationship curriculum with their junior high kids. They've told me that although they sometimes have awkward silent moments, the youth and their parents appreciate the openness and inclusion of a biblical outlook about sex and the self-esteem issues that come with puberty.

If we're afraid to talk about self-image and a biblical understanding of sex, our youth are going to get their information from somewhere else—and one of the most skewed outlooks on gender issues is found right in your own home. In the book *Oral Sex Is the New Goodnight Kiss: The Sexual Bullying of Girls*, Sharlene Azam argues that objectified girls and their acceptance of being objectified is only natural based on their lifestyle and the activities of those around them.

> When a young girl's beliefs about relationships are influenced by pornography; when her online friends decide if she's "hot or not"; when a girl's ideas about her lifestyle and how she should be treaded are derived from MTV; when the magazines she reads feature stories about collagen shots for "G-spot amplification"; when her mother takes pole dancing lessons to unleash her "inner stripper"; and her father watches Naked News on his mobile, being objectified seems normal.[72]

---

[72] Azam, Sharlene. *Oral Sex Is the New Goodnight Kiss: The Sexual Bullying of Girls* (Santa Monica, CA: Sharlene Azam, 2008), p. 3.

When it comes to the over-sexualization of teen girls, there is one clear message: "I am ready to be consumed."

> Drunk, underage girls bare their breasts in Girls Gone Wild videos. T-shirts for girls read "Porn Star", "The Rumors are True" and "I know what Boys Want" across the chest. Sweat pants have "juicy", "yummy" and "sweet" printed across the backside. The current brand identity for girls is clear: "I am something to be consumed."[73]

I think it's a pretty fair assumption to say that this consumed lifestyle starts with TV.

Sexuality in Thirty Minutes or Less

How many TV shows do you watch per week? There are so many TV shows today, not to mention all the shows available per season on DVD. Do you watch any of these? What do you watch regularly? How many hours do you watch per night?

TV SHOW	WHAT YOU WATCH	HOURS SPENT
Two and a Half Men		
How I Met Your Mother		

---

[73] Ibid.

TV SHOW	WHAT YOU WATCH	HOURS SPENT
Desperate Housewives		
Skins		
Pretty Little Liars		
Jersey Shore		
The Big Bang Theory		
Glee		
Mad Men		
Modern Family		

What about *Two and a Half Men*?

If you have seen it, I want you to watch it again. You can actually do this next activity with any of the shows you watch... and you might be surprised. Watch the show with a pad of paper and a pencil. I want you to record every time you see or hear something that is sexual in reference. I think you will be surprised at your final outcome. I know I was.

I have actually found between 50 and 75 sexual references in one episode. The show is only 22–24 minutes long! At the end of the episode, I want you to look at the page and ask yourself what kind of shows you actually like.

If it is shows like *Two and a Half Men,* then you like shows about sex, because this show is about one thing—sex. Two characters who are trying to get sex and a son who says things he probably shouldn't.

Jersey Shore is usually in the Nielson Top Ten for cable TV. One of its stars, Snooki (her real name is Nicole Polizzi), has said that she shouldn't be a role model. People Magazine Online posted an article about Snooki's visit to *The Ellen DeGeneres Show:*

> "Now when you say if you didn't black out it's a good night for you, are you serious?" DeGeneres asks the reality star.
>
> Snooki replies, "Yes because I want to remember my night and sometimes I just don't. It sucks. So you're like, What did I do? Why did I wake up in a garbage can?"
>
> DeGeneres laughs and asks how often the reality star finds herself in that position, to which Snooki says, "Oh, like once a month."
>
> Later in the interview, DeGeneres points out that "the blacking out thing isn't a good example" for teen fans, and Snooki shoots back: "Well, I don't want to be a role model."[74]

There are more than a couple of things wrong with this interview. First of all, she's a role model whether she wants to be one or not. That's what happens when you're on a TV show. Second, she's promoting alcoholism and drinking

---

[74] Hammel, Sara. "Snooki: Passing Out in a Garbage Can Sucks," http://www.people.com/people/article/0,,20455059,00.html (accessed January 26, 2011).

as a way to get past her problems. She's not only alluding to the fact that drinking can help with her problems, but she also says it's a way to forget her problems. *Jersey Shore* is one of the most popular shows on TV, and these are the types of messages that are at the core of the show.

Obviously, *Two and a Half Men* and *Jersey* Shore are not the only shows like this. *90210* had an oral sex scene in the first ten minutes and *Gossip Girl* has even featured a threesome. The creators and marketers of *Gossip Girl*, when they released their new ads featuring the acronym O.M.F.G., knew they were marketing sex to teens and tweens. Yet in interviews these creators describe their ads as "well-written headlines that are provocative and would catch our viewers' attention... and, in a tongue-in-cheek way, capture what the show is about."[75] The show is about sex and what passions the writers can manipulate the best. These writers are trying to teach that these are normal teenage lives, but normal lives should not look anything like this. Take that same chart we filled out above and do the same thing, but this time instead of filling in the hours spent watching TV, fill in the number of sexual references you hear or see.

TV SHOW	SEXUAL REFERENCES	SHOW LENGTH
Two and a Half Men	50–75	22–24 minutes

[75] People, "OMG! Check out the sexy new Gossip Girl Ads," *TV Watch*, July 23, 2008, http://tvwatch.people.com/2008/07/23/omg-check-out-the-new-gossip-girl-ads/ (accessed July 3, 2010).

TV SHOW	SEXUAL REFERENCES	SHOW LENGTH
How I Met Your Mother		
Desperate Housewives		
Skins		
Pretty Little Liars		
Jersey Shore		
The Big Bang Theory		
Glee		
Mad Men		
Modern Family		

How are shows all about sex working for you?

How do shows about sex relate your ancient faith to your modern world?

The Parents Television Council recently released a new study entitled "Sexualized Teen Girls: Tinsel Town's New Target." This study was conducted by enlisting the top twenty-five shows from the Nielson ranking for 12–17-year-olds. The shows included *The Office*, *NCIS*, *Two and a Half Men*, *The Big Bang Theory*, *The Vampire Diaries*, *Grey's*

Anatomy, Desperate Housewives, Lost, Family Guy, House, Glee, The Cleveland Show, American Dad, and *The Simpsons.*[76] In order to understand what they're talking about, let's look at the definition of the word "sexualized":

- a person's value comes only from his or her sexual appeal or sexual behaviour, to the exclusion of other characteristics;
- a person is held to a standard that equates physical attractiveness (narrowly defined) with being sexy;
- a person is sexually objectified—that is, made into a thing for others' sexual use—rather than seen as a person with the capacity for independent action and decision making; and/or
- sexuality is inappropriately imposed upon a person. (Especially relevant to children).[77]

The fact is that this study continues to show that over-sexualized teens and over-sexualized content is the new norm. How often have you wondered, *Why is she dressed like that? That isn't acceptable.* If you work with teens or have teens in your house, a phrase like that has probably run through your head at some point or another, and one of the reasons is that this is normal. Have a look at some of the findings:

---

[76] Parents Television Council. "Sexualized Teen Girls: Tinsel Town's New Target," http://www.parentstv.org/FemaleSexualization/Study.htm (accessed November 28, 2010).
[77] Ibid.

- Underage female characters are shown participating in a higher percentage of sexualizing depictions compared to adults (47% and 29% respectively). The majority of scenes featuring adult female characters involved verbal sexual references. Underage depictions consisted of implied nudity and/or sexual gestures (suggestive dancing, erotic kissing, erotic touching, and/or implied intercourse).
- Only 5% of the underage female characters communicated any form of dislike for being sexualized (excluding scenes depicting healthy sexuality).
- 67% of the episodes involving sexualized scenes of underage girls were in a comedic genre (comedies and/or animated series). Further examination revealed that 73% of the sexual incidents (excluding relationships that represented "healthy" sexuality) were presented in a humorous manner designed to evoke laughter.

It becomes clear what kind of damage these messages can do when you consider that these young girls are searching for answers to questions like "Who am I? What am I good at? Why doesn't so-and-so like me?" The show *Pretty Little Liars* has even been described by some of its cast as the *Desperate Housewives* for a younger generation. *The*

New York Post reviewed the show and established a strong argument against the show's content:

> So why will you hate it? For all the reasons you probably love *Desperate Housewives*. Within the first 15 minutes, the following takes place: Underage Aria (Lucy Hale) fools around with her new English teacher. 16-year-old Hanna (Ashley Benson) steals designer glasses from the mall. Spencer (Troian Bellisario) gets a bikini massage from her older sister's fiancé. And Emily (Shay Mitchell) smokes weed and toys with having her first lesbian experience with the new girl in the group, Maya (Bianca Lawson). So no, *Pretty Little Liars* isn't exactly *Little House on the Prairie*. It's more a melding of *Housewives*, *Gossip Girl* and *Twilight*... Ok, so we've established that there is no socially redeeming value in this series and that your kids shouldn't watch it if they are too young and impressionable...[78]

All that being said, the young women we work with as leaders have probably either seen the show or read the books it's based on, by Sara Shepherd.

Here's what the *Post* article does not tell you. Almost every girl we encounter will relate to one of the four main characters in the *Pretty Little Liars* universe. Aria is going through strong identity issues as she tries to find the perfect "Aria."

---

[78] Stasi, Linda. "New York Post Review," http://www.nypost.com/p/entertainment/not_just_another_pretty_face_DrC d5xm3FCdl1FZosgZel (accessed January 30, 2011).

> Trouble was Aria wasn't sure who Aria was. Since
> turning eleven, she'd tried out punk Aria, artsy
> Aria, documentary film Aria, and, right before
> they moved she'd even tried ideal Rosewood girl
> Aria, the horse-riding, polo-shirt-wearing, Coach-
> satchel-toting girl who was everything Rosewood
> boys loved but everything Arai wasn't.[79]

Identity issues also surround the character of Emily. Her parents have taught her that character is built from the inside and not what you wear or show off:

> ...she never wore anything tight or remotely cute
> like the rest of the girls in her seventh-grade
> class...[80]

However, like most preteens, Emily is starting to question and wonder what sexual identity really is.

> Emily also felt a little self-conscious about her
> body, which was strong, muscular, and not as
> slender as it used to be. She didn't usually feel so
> aware of herself, even when she was in her
> swimsuit, which was practically naked."[81]

Emily begins to question her looks and self-image as she struggles with her own sexuality and her own feelings towards Maya.

Hanna struggles with identity issues as well. Hanna used to be overweight, but she found a way to lose it all.

---

[79] Shepherd, Sara. *Pretty Little Liars* (New York, NY: HarperCollins, 2006), p. 39.
[80] Ibid., p. 10.
[81] Ibid., p. 79.

> While hard core dieting was sexy and admirable,
> there was nothing, *nothing*, glamorous about
> eating a ton of fatty, greasy, preferably cheese-
> filled crap and then puking it all up.[82]

Hanna's eating disorder is an attempt to gain her estranged father's attention, just like her shoplifting addiction and her attempt to have sex with her boyfriend. Hanna's issues come from a lack of attention and a daughter's need for her father's love and acceptance.

Spencer is dealing with an issue that is becoming a danger in many households today: competition between siblings to win parents' attention. Spencer feels that the only way to succeed in life is through constant commitments. Time doesn't seem to be an issue for Spencer, but we all know that eventually all teens will burn out.

> In just two days, Spencer was starting her junior
> year at Rosewood and would have to surrender
> herself to this year's jam-packed schedule: Five
> Aps, leadership training, charity drive organizing,
> yearbook editing, drama tryouts, hockey
> practice, and sending in summer program
> applications ASAP, since everyone knew the best
> way to get into an Ivy was to get into one of their
> pre-college summer camps.[83]

I think we can look at these four characters and use them to identify a young person we work with, someone

---

[82] Ibid., p. 51.
[83] Ibid., p. 93.

who struggles with identity by making themselves something they're not.

We also know of youth who are struggling with questions surrounding their sexuality. These questions in particular can lead to isolation because of a fear of being bullied or made fun of. Characters like Emily from *Pretty Little Liars* or Kurt from *Glee* are going to resonate with youth who are questioning their sexuality, because they see their lives being played out in front of them. Our young people will base their decisions on what they see Kurt or Emily do.

As leaders, we also know youth who are struggling with self-injury, and we'll talk about that in more detail a bit later in the book. What about the youth who are overcommitting themselves and burning out because that's the only path to success they know?

TV has a strong influence over the youth we work with. Whether it's issues of sexuality, gender roles, or what love really is, TV has a strong voice in helping them form their worldviews.

Check out some of these resources, which cover the sexualization of youth culture.

- *Mean Girls*, by Hayley DiMarco (Grand Rapids, MI: Revell, 2004)
- *Almost Sex*, by Hayley DiMarco (Grand Rapids, MI: Revell/Hungary Planet, 2009)
- *B4U D8*, by Hayley DiMarco (Grand Rapids, MI: Revell, 2009)

- *Technical Virgin,* by Hayley DiMarco (Grand Rapids, MI: Revell, 2008)
- *Cinderella Ate My Daughter,* by Peggy Orenstein (New York, NY: HarperCollins, 2011)
- *Lolita Effect,* by M. Gigi Durham, Ph.D. (Woodstock, NY: Overlook Press, 2008)
- *Oral Sex Is the New Goodnight Kiss: The Sexual Bullying of Girls,* by Sharlene Azam (Santa Monica, CA: Sharlene Azam, 2008)
- *Queen Bees and WannaBees,* by Rosalind Wiseman (New York, NY: Crown Publishers, 2002)
- *Sex Has a Price Tag: Discussions About Sexuality, Spirituality and Self-Respect,* by Pam Stenzel and Crystal Kirgiss (Grand Rapids, MI: Zondervan, 2003)
- *Nobody Told Me,* by Pam Stenzel (Ventura, CA: Regal, 2010)

Unrated Movies for All Ages

Movies are no different.

I could list hundreds and hundreds of movies that have come out in the past, in the present, or are soon to be released that focus on sex. Would you watch a movie that is full of the following topics and values?

Sexual slang, including many crude anatomical references, abounds. Sex-related dialogue also includes topics ranging from pubic hair on teenage boys to elderly women using sex toys. Anal and oral sex, orgasms, masturbation, pornography, tampons, losing one's virginity, genital size and "loud, intense make-up sex" also garner verbal attention.[84]

How about these values?

More than 200 f-words. More than 50 s-words. Jesus' name is abused a handful of times; God's more than 20, sometimes coupled with "d––n." "Lord" is prefaced with the f-word. Other language includes "c––k," "d––k," "p–––y," "b––ch," "t–ts" and "douche bag." Slurs include "faggot" and "queer." Several obscene gestures are made.[85]

How about one more? This film is the most recent of the three.

Months before it arrived in theaters, Ashton Kutcher reported that the production title for *No Strings Attached* was the much more direct *F––– Buddies*. Indeed, Adam and Emma are seen

---

[84] Keffer, Lindy. "Video Reviews: *I Love You, Man*," *Focus on the Family's Plugged In Online*,
http://www.pluggedin.com/videos/2009/q2/iloveyouman.aspx (accessed August 10, 2010).
[85] Whitmore, Meredith with Steven Isaac. "Video Reviews: *Hot Tub Time Machine*," *Focus on the Family's Plugged In Online*,
http://www.pluggedin.ca/videos/2010/q2/hottubtimemachine.aspx (accessed January 30, 2011).

in the throes of intercourse in several scenes and a variety of locales, incorporating very realistic movements and sounds. One scene ends in a clench-mouthed orgasm. In fact, their vocal expressiveness is even joked about as Adam's roommate calls out, "I can't concentrate on my porn with all this real sex going on!"...

"Emma wants a relationship without the relationship," actress Natalie Portman told Fox News. "She just wants the sex. It's unusual but funny. I love romantic comedies, but I'm tired of seeing girls who want to get married all the time and that's all they're interested in. I think there is a wider vision of how women can conduct their lives and what they want."...

Apparently screenwriter Elizabeth Meriwether and director Ivan Reitman agree. And so their film sports a grinning anomie, showcases uninhibited trysts, and doesn't blush a bit about the sex-and-go worldview it supports amidst one-liners and love-lost sighs...

It does at least come around to mildly admitting that it can be difficult to have noncommittal sex without a few pesky emotions getting in the way. And it speculates that adults who pursue a me-centered life will negatively impact themselves and their offspring. But it certainly doesn't suggest that you should change your ways. In fact, if anything, there's a much more focused encouragement here for young and old alike to find their own paths through the "no rules/new rules" of dating and sexuality.[86]

---

[86] Hoose, Bob. "Video Reviews: *No Strings Attached,*" *Focus on the Family's Plugged In Online,*

The fact is, you probably have seen these movies. The films were *I Love You, Man, Hot Tub Time Machine,* and *No Strings Attached.* After one talk, a kid came up to me and asked if I was talking about the Unrated or Restricted version of *I Love You, Man.* I said it didn't really matter, nor did I particularly care what version the film was.

The boy, he was in Grade Seven.

He said he had seen both and didn't know which one I was talking about.

I really didn't know where to go with a kid that young.

"Ruder, cruder, and nuder"—How do you connect your faith with that?

When a film is labeled unrated, do we really understand what it is saying? Some parents think, "Oh, it hasn't been rated yet." What it really means is that they pulled stuff out of it to get it a restricted rating. They will actual pull item-by-item, scene-by-scene, and object-by-object until they get the right rating. Then they throw it all back in and place it in Blockbuster.

The questions we need to ask about films like *No Strings Attached* and *Friends with Benefits,* starring Mila Kunis and Justin Timberlake, are these: what's being taught to our youth about relationships? What values are being promoted?

We now have films promoting the idea that casual sex between friends is a good idea. It doesn't matter how the plot plays out, or whether the actors get together or not, because the idea and worldview is already placed before them.

---

http://www.pluggedin.ca/videos/2010/q2/hottubtimemachine.aspx (accessed January 30, 2011).

The concept of "friends with benefits" is already a huge issue in teen culture. It promotes a worldview that leads to someone's feelings getting hurt when they become emotionally involved in the relationship. Many films pushed the boundaries this year in terms of the definition of a relationship and sexual encounters. *Black Swan*, featuring Natalie Portman and Mila Kunis, has a very steamy sexual scene between the two.

Love and Other Drugs is the story of a Viagra salesman who meets a girl who doesn't want to be tied down to a relationship, but they fall victim to love in the end. The story is not the issue; the issue is the casual nature of the sex scenes within the movie. Director Ed Zwick used the sex scenes as a way to communicate the characters' lives and expressions. In an interview with *Newsweek*, he described this process:

> Sex is a way of communicating in life. Sex is an expression. It should be understood in the context of the story, to be part of the narrative... You understand that the scene has a beginning, a middle, and an end. It has a purpose. In this movie, sex plays an important role in the narrative arc of the characters—they fall into bed long before they fall into love. That was our guide... How funny that we wouldn't consider sex part of a love story. In my experience, it's a rather central part of anybody's love.[87]

[87] Setoodeh, Ramin. "What You Need to Know About Shooting a Sex Scene." *The Daily Beast*, November 17, 2010, http://www.thedailybeast.com/newsweek/blogs/pop-vox/2010/11/17/love-

Sex should be central to people's love stories only when they are married, especially if you live and teach a biblical worldview. If we're living in a biblical worldview, the messages these movies are giving our children, for the most part, teach them quite the opposite.

The new way that movies are being butchered is through something called a "Producer's Cut." In my time, it was Oliver Stone redoing *Pearl Harbor* in a different way. He would edit and change the ending. Now they take a woman, naked, and walk her back and forth in front of a blue screen. They then add her to the movie.

That isn't a "producer's cut." That is nudity for the sake of nudity.

I actually had someone ask me what *Zack and Miri Make a Porno* was about. It is about Zack and Miri making a porno! Do you really need to ask me what it is about? It is a new love story, right? They fall in love after they have sex in a movie. Director Kevin Smith, when faced with a NC-17 rating, argued his way down to a simple R rating.

> Look, if I were a 13-year-old boy, and I saw [*Zack and Miri Make a Porno*] on cable back in 1983? Yes, it would [make me masturbate]. Now, as a 13-year-old boy, if I saw this movie? It would not titillate me. I would simply go to the Internet and watch real people having real sex. How can you possibly say this is too erotically charged when it's so obviously a comedy with people having

and-other-drugs-director-ed-zwick-on-how-to-shoot-a-sex-scene-with-actors-anne-hathaway-and-jake-gyllenhaal.htm (accessed November 17, 2010).

over-the-top fake sex, when we can see examples
of real sex at a keystroke?[88]

Kevin Smith used today's acceptance of porn as a logical
defense for his film's final rating.

For the first time ever this year, we had a date rape
scene in a movie which we now call funny. *Observe and
Report*, with Seth Rogen. He's on a bed having sex with a
passed-out woman, who has puked... that's called date rape.
I deal with date rape about a hundred times a year. I deal
with the suicide, cutting, hurt, and pain that comes along
with that. The woman wakes up and says, "Did I not tell
you to stop, mother f—er?" And we call it funny. The
actress even said in an interview that she didn't know where
that was going to go.

So when we were shooting it, even the date-rape
scene—or as I refer to it, "The Tender Love-
Making Scene"—I just thought, "We'll shoot it,
but it's not gonna be in the movie. I don't have to
worry about that one." And yet there it is... I've
got this all wrong. I don't understand the tone of
this movie at all. I think it's really difficult for an
actor to get a sense of that when you aren't a
part of the project from the beginning.[89]

[88] Smith, Kevin. "Culture Clips," *Focus on the Families Plugged In Online*,
October 13, 2008,
http://www.pluggedin.com/cultureclips/2008/october132008.aspx (accessed
August 10, 2010).
[89] Tobias, Scott. "Interview Anna Farris," *A.V. Club*, April 7, 2009,
http://www.avclub.com/articles/anna-faris,26245/ (accessed July 5, 2010).

Movies have changed when even the actors begin to question the reasoning behind the script, the tone, and even the grand scheme of the films they are in.

Parents must draw a line. When did we give up on our kids? I think many parents need to grow up, because many parents today don't seem to parent at all. This is generalizing a bit, because I know there are some good parents out there, but I see more and more parents who think they are good parents, but they're not.

Here's an interview conducted by Vibe Magazine with rapper Young Jeezy. When asked if his son will respect him, this is his answer:

> Hell, no. He's how I was when I was younger—but a little sharper... I wanna be (a good father), but it's hard because of the things that I say and the things that I represent. I can only imagine how his teachers feel. Even though I am taking to him, I'm still just on the other end of the phone. I tell him every time I talk to him that I'm not ashamed of who I am. My son's seen me locked up, f—ed up. I lay around and think maybe I'm sacrificing the wrong end. Maybe I should have sacrificed this for him. It crosses my mind a lot, but I don't know.[90]

We know weak parents. The problem parents are the ones who think they're strong when they really aren't. They're the parents in our church and in our communities who think they've got it together, but they don't. We have

---

[90] Meadows-Ingram, Benjamin. "Can't Tell Me Nothin'," *Vibe Magazine*, October 2008, p. 86–87.

to ask the same questions Young Jeezy wrestles with in that interview. What TV shows, movies, and song lyrics are we allowing to influence us and the people around us?

What is the most disturbing movie you have ever seen?

I have asked over 200,000 people this question in about three years and three people have agreed with me and said that the most disturbing movie they have seen is *Transformers. Transformers* was a concept originally made for my generation. Growing up, I would leave basketball practice, run home, and watch *Transformers*. When I tell people that, I usually get inhales. People cannot believe that the most disturbing movie for me is *Transformers*. I say, watch it again with a piece of paper and write down all the sexual innuendos. I had one question when I saw the first *Transformers* film: why was a five-year-old beside me on opening night in a booster seat?

In my mind, I actually looked at the dad and said, "You're an idiot." Honestly, he's five. It is a PG-13 movie; it says so right on the trailer. An organization that knows nothing about Christ says you should probably be thirteen to watch this. It has sexuality and violence written right on it. As I am thinking these lovely yet inappropriate thoughts, the whole row in front of me fills with Grade One students and the row behind me fills up with Grade Two kids. How do I know that the pornification of culture, mentioned earlier, is done? It is done when we are giving the discussion of masturbation to kindergarten kids. My kids are six and seven and hardly understand sexuality, let alone talking about what masturbation is. The same can be said about the discussion in the film about the porn magazine called Busty Beauties.

Megan Fox is being used in these films as a form of eye candy. She does not act or say anything of relevance, and yet she is okay with that. In an interview with *Entertainment Weekly*, she was asked about her experience of being a "club girl" in the movie *Bad Boys*, what it was like and how she felt about being used. "I thought it was awesome. I was going to a Christian high school and I wasn't a feminist yet. I hadn't sat back and analyzed society yet. I was 15! I just did what I was told to do."[91] It is like *Baywatch* redone. She just runs for half the film. She hardly has any lines and does basically nothing. In the second film, she is drawing and you can't even see what she is doing. The goal was to see up the back of her jeans.

What is interesting about Megan Fox is that she feels this should be every girl's dream. In the same interview, when asked about purely being a sex symbol actress, she says it is empowering.

> It doesn't bother me. I don't know why someone would complain about that. That just means that the bar has been set pretty low. People don't expect me to do anything that's worth watching. So I can only be an overachiever. I think all women in Hollywood are known as sex symbols. That's what our purpose is in this business. You're merchandised, you're a product. You're sold and it's based on sex. But that's okay. I think

---

[91] Nashawaty, Chris. "Megan Fox: 'Fallen' Angel," *Entertainment Weekly*, June 10, 2009, http://www.ew.com/ew/article/0,,20284375,00.html (accessed April 15, 2010).

women should be empowered by that, not
degraded.[92]

The message she gives in *Transformers* is the same
message she gives in reality. Set your bar low and rely on
beauty to get you what you need.
I was recently asked by someone why his kids were
swearing so much. I explained as easily as I could, "Well,
my kids watch films like *Bolt* and *Madagascar.* Your kids are
watching *Scary Movie 4,* and they are in kindergarten and
Grade Two. Your son has watched *Watchmen* and you
bought *Transformers* for your kindergarten son." My kids
might hear "Bum" from time to time, and they think fart is
a bad word. Go figure! One day, my daughter Zoe came
home from school and informed me that she now knew the
F-word. I hesitated for a moment and then asked her what
she had learned.
"Fart," she sheepishly told me. To her, that is a bad
word because in her context, based on her age and the
media in her life, that's as bad as it gets. Why do we need to
expose children to excessive violence and sexuality before
they can even understand what it is all about? Does a
kindergarten student understand what a porn magazine is, or
masturbation for that matter? So why are we allowing them
to watch movies that speak so openly about those topics?
Is the new normal to expose ourselves to topics before
we understand what they are all about?

---

[92] Ibid.

I will not let my son watch *Transformers*, and it is hard because I do not think there is a single friend of his who has not seen it.

It is time that we begin to ask ourselves what values we are picking up from the films we watch.

When *Transformers 2* was released, I pulled into the parking lot of the theatre and prayed, "God, please don't give me content for my talks at the movie. I don't care for more content." I just hoped that the crazy parenting experience of the first film would not repeat itself and that I could just watch. I sat down with my drink and popcorn and took a look around. To my astonishment, there was only one other man and woman. That was it. There was just one problem, though. I couldn't figure out why the theatre was so loud. Then I saw the twenty-three four-year-olds between the man and woman. It was a birthday party and I literally sat with tears in my eyes and filled nine pages of notes on my iPhone. Here is a sample of what the audience was exposed to during *Transformers 2*:

- "Kiss this, b★★★★!"
- "I'm gonna skinny dip and you can say s★★★ about it."
- "It's an a★★ kicking!"
- "Park my foot in you're a★★!"
- "That's my eye, you crazy b★★★★!"
- "Had sex with her in my dream."
- "Pop a cap in his a★★."
- "He's an a★★hole!"

- "Oh s★★★!"
- "I am directly below the enemy scrotum."

I have three issues with *Transformers*.

- You and I think it is normal. We just go see movies and we do not question what we are taking in. Everything becomes normal.
- Students think it is normal. They don't gasp when I put it up on the screen. If you gasp at content like this, realize that they've been so desensitized that it's normal now.
- The writers. Michael Bay does not write this film alone. He sits down with a team of writers. My question is, who sits down as a team and decides to put testicles on a robot? I don't remember that in the original cartoon. How about the line, "I'm directly below the enemy scrotum"? Who thought that should go in? Is it necessary? How does it pass through a team of writers, multiple viewings, and still end up in the final cut of the film? If those are some of the best ideas you can come up with, then you are a pathetic writer and should switch jobs.

There are a million things to talk about in films like *Transformers*, because no one walks out of a movie and says, "I just loved the discussion on masturbation." Those types of discussions are irrelevant, yet many of the films we watch are just laced with this type of material. I have friends who have recently seen films like *Sex and the City 2* and *Kick Ass* and sat through them with tweens and their parents.

Kick Ass came out this year to very mixed reviews. Comic fans loved and hated it and critics did not know how to take Chloë Grace Moretz and her Hit Girl alter ego. One of her main lines in the film is, "I never play." This would not be so bad if she wasn't at an age where she should be enjoying the innocence of preteen life. However, these are very fitting words from Hit Girl in the movie and I found them to be some of the most chilling.

> As an eleven-year-old actor and character in the film, the actions of Hit Girl are disturbing, to say the least. She is the main killer in the movie and has no regard for human life whatsoever. The message that comes through her actions is a desensitized one. Killing isn't a game in this movie; it's second nature. There is one scene shot from the same angle and viewpoint of a single person shooter, sort of like the one that *007: Golden Eye* (for Nintendo 64) made famous. We are also shown a filmed execution that gets played over the Internet. In an age when we witness this on the news, do we really need to see it in a movie? Does this give the message that nothing shocks us as a culture anymore?[93]

---

[93] Clarke, Adam B.R. "Kick Ass Review," http://www.theemergingnetwork.com/The_Emerging_Network/Narrative/Entries/2010/4/27_Kick_Ass_Review.html (accessed: January 29, 2011).

Has media, especially movies, become the one indulgence we allow in our lives? Do we look past everything that contradicts our biblical worldview?

How about *Iron Man* and the stripper pole on the plane, or the multitude of scantily clad "cheerleaders" during the opening of *Iron Man 2*? The latest *Crank* film had only one sequence that was not filled with blood, gore, skin, sex, or profanity—and it only lasted about ninety seconds.

The Bible is quite clear, yet we do not talk about Mark 9:42 often: *"On the other hand, if you give one of these simple, childlike believers a hard time, bullying or taking advantage of their simple trust, you'll soon wish you hadn't. You'd be better off dropped in the middle of the lake with a millstone around your neck."* This is a direct warning about causing young people to sin. I think many writers, directors, producers, and actors in Hollywood, Vancouver, and Toronto need to take these words to heart. The actions and values played out in their films are influential to all of us, yet many times they go unquestioned. We also need to take these words to heart and realize we are being manipulated into thinking this is normal; once we think it is normal, we fall away from the ancient faith we are trying to follow.

However, the people in the industry aren't the only ones to blame. You have to be honest with yourself about the content you show your kids at home and on youth retreats. Take a look at Ephesians 6:4: *"Fathers, don't exasperate your children by coming down hard on them. Take them by the hand and lead them in the way of the Master."* This is my favourite verse about being a father. It keeps me asking, what am I introducing into my kids' lives?

Sexuality is a huge conversation and Ephesians 5:3–4 is a great place to start. *"Don't allow love to turn into lust, setting off a downhill slide into sexual promiscuity, filthy practices, or bullying greed. Though some tongues just love the taste of gossip, those who follow Jesus have better uses for language than that. Don't talk dirty or silly. That kind of talk doesn't fit our style. Thanksgiving is our dialect."* There's more to sex than mere skin on skin. Sex is as much a spiritual mystery as a physical act. As written in Scripture, the two become one. *"We must not pursue the kind of sex that avoids commitment and intimacy, leaving us more lonely than ever—the kind of sex that can never 'become one'"* (1 Corinthians 6:16–18).

A student said to me recently, "Can my girlfriend give me oral sex or not?"

The fact is this: we want a yes or no answer, and that's it. Not some line about how it's not about what we *can* do sexually, like it says in Ephesians, because that is too confusing for us to interpret. The question should not be how close you can get to your guy/girlfriend, but how close you can get to God in your relationships.

Let's take a look at the downward slide. It starts with holding hands, which leads to kissing, which eventually leads to oral sex and intercourse. First, I want to say that holding hands is fine and I say that because I have to. I have to because I deal with suicide attempts all the time involving people who have said that if you touch a girl before you are married you are sinning before God.

A guy once came up to me weeping—not just crying—and says this in between weeps: "Girlfriend... beach... parents... sex..."

Okay, so he got caught by his parents on the beach having sex. It seemed easy enough to decipher. This interpretation, however, wasn't even close.

He was on a beach in northern Ontario walking with his girlfriend. Her parents were behind them holding hands. Then his girlfriend reaches down... and at this point I pause, but it's okay. She grabs his hand.

"Okay," was my response.

"Brett, I read a book that said if you touch a girl before you marry you are sinning before the God you love." As the conversation continued, he said, "I had my first suicide attempt that week." The day I got to him was his second suicide attempt and he was ready to try for the third time.

There are times when I just don't know what to say. I said, "When my daughter is in Grade Seven or Eight and she is walking on the beach holding hands and I am behind her, I pray for that every day of my life." His shoulders shrunk right down and he started to cry. The guilt placed upon kids is amazing. Holding hands is nice, but everything else is a problem.

The Bible is very clear when it says to flee from sexual immorality. It is the only place in the Bible I can think of where it says to more than merely not do something; it actually says to *flee and run* from sexual immorality.

Sexual immorality is defined as being sexually fulfilled in any way, shape, or form with anybody other than your spouse, whether you are married or not. It includes sex, oral sex, and masturbation. Read 1 Corinthians 6:14–20.

> God honored the Master's body by raising it
> from the grave. He'll treat yours with the same
> resurrection power. Until that time, remember
> that your bodies are created with the same
> dignity as the Master's body. You wouldn't take
> the Master's body off to a whorehouse, would
> you? I should hope not.
>
> There's more to sex than mere skin on skin.
> Sex is as much spiritual mystery as physical fact.
> As written in Scripture, "The two become one."
> Since we want to become spiritually one with the
> Master, we must not pursue the kind of sex that
> avoids commitment and intimacy, leaving us
> more lonely than ever—the kind of sex that can
> never "become one." There is a sense in which
> sexual sins are different from all others. In sexual
> sin we violate the sacredness of our own bodies,
> these bodies that were made for God-given and
> God-modeled love, for "becoming one" with
> another. Or didn't you realize that your body is a
> sacred place, the place of the Holy Spirit? Don't
> you see that you can't live however you please,
> squandering what God paid such a high price
> for? The physical part of you is not some piece
> of property belonging to the spiritual part of
> you. God owns the whole works. So let people
> see God in and through your body.

I have had students ask me, "What about foreplay?" Be careful of this slippery slope, because even before you begin going down it, you give away your heart. We give away our hearts very quickly to people we really do not even know. Oftentimes we give it to people who will only be close to us for a short period of time. Sexual immorality covers much in the middle portion of that slope and the whole middle section is foreplay. Foreplay is designed to get you excited for sex.

Dr. Louann Brizendine explains why it is so easy to fall down the slope.

> If testosterone were beer, a 9-year-old boy would be getting the equivalent of a cup a day. But a 15-year-old would be getting the equivalent of two gallons a day. This fuels their sexual engines and makes it impossible for them to stop thinking about female body parts and sex.[94]

These developing hormones are uncharted territory for most young males. That is why understanding the differences between desire, lust, and biblical love is essential. Without knowledge, one cannot help but fall down the slippery slope of desire.

What makes you different from the millions of other people who cannot stop themselves from sliding down that slippery slope? In my fourteen years of speaking, almost all the students who hit the bottom of the slide say they regret it.

If we really want to avoid saying "I wish I didn't," we need to come up with some practical things to help us not go down this slide.

I tell guys all the time, "Don't lie on a couch with your girlfriend lying down in front of you."

---

[94] Brizendine, Dr. Louann. "Love, sex and the male brain," *CNN Opinion*, March 25, 2010, http://www.cnn.com/2010/OPINION/03/23/brizendine.male.brain/index.html ?hpt=C2 (accessed August 10, 2010).

For a guy, having his girlfriend lying down in front of him will turn him on incredibly. So just don't do it. Don't lie down anywhere. Just sit up. If you are going to struggle with being alone, then don't surround yourselves with things that will help you slide down that slippery slope.

"Don't excite love, don't stir it up, until the time is ripe—and you're ready" (Song of Solomon 8:4).

The same needs to be said to us, the older generation. We need to start taking care of our own marriages. I think the book *Jim & Casper Go to Church* says it pretty cut and dry: "Stop having sex with people you aren't married to."[95]

Rob Bell, in his book *Sex God*, makes a connection between our sexuality and spirituality. This is a connection that cannot be breached, because both ends are intertwined in their meaning, understanding, and creation.

> ...but they're at this point in their relationship where issues like trust and commitment and future and kids and marriage are starting to linger in their minds and hearts, and underneath it all they both have this question: "Are you the one?" But neither of them has actually voiced it, and both of them experienced their parents divorcing at a young age, so anytime the subject of marriage comes up, things get confusing and tense very quickly... Something deeper. Something behind it all. You can't talk about sexuality without talking about how we are made. And that will inevitably lead to who made us. At

---

[95] Henderson, Jim and Matt Casper. *Jim & Casper Go To Church: Frank Conversation About Faith, Churches, and Well Meaning Christians* (Carol Stream, IL: Barna Books, 2007), p. 99.

some point you need to talk about God. Sex.
God. They're connected. And they can't be
separated. Where one is, you will always find the
other.[96]

Our relationships are under the microscope. The youth
that surround us are watching us and using our example in
deciding who to engage in their future relationships. We
have all heard the stories of pastors' lives being destroyed by
bad relationship choices, right? We need to start acting our
age and being responsible to the ones we love. That also
means that our partners cannot, as Bell points out, turn into
a "that."

The problem is that "that" is actually a "she." A
person. A woman. With a name, a history, with
feelings. It seems harmless until you're that girl—
and then it hurts. It's degrading. It's violating. It
does something to a person's soul. Jesus had
much to say about what happens when a woman,
an image-bearer, a carrier of the divine spark,
becomes a "that." In the book of Matthew, Jesus
teaches that "anyone who looks lustfully has
already committed adultery with her in his
heart." He connects our eyes and our intentions
and our thoughts with the state of our hearts.[97]

What does that mean to us? It means that we have to
put the same barriers in our lives that we expect our youth
to use. If you struggle with porn, use a PVR for late-night

[96] Bell, Rob. *Sex God: Exploring the Endless Connections Between Sexuality and Spirituality* (Grand Rapids, MI: Zondervan, 2007), p. 15.
[97] Ibid., p. 20.

TV viewing, or an online filter that emails your closest friends a list of the sites you're visiting.

When I travel, I refuse to be picked up or dropped off by any woman who's not my wife, Dawn. That's a barrier I have put up in my life to help keep me from crashing. Sex wasn't intended to crash our marriages; it was intended to be a God-given gift. Genesis 1–2 tells us that God created men and women to be in a relationship, to be one flesh, to reproduce. Then he called it all good.

Community and accountability are essential if we want to save our relationships. When you're accountable to your spouse, your marriage becomes less about you and more about the intermixing of your relationship, sexuality, and spirituality. If we're asking our kids to enter into a biblical worldview and exit out of a highly sexualized and violent worldview, the first place we need to look is the state of our marriages.

In the fall of 2008, Mark Driscoll did a sermon series on Song of Songs entitled "The Peasant Princess." It's a good resource for husbands and wives to work through together.

> Through the story of the Peasant Princess, we can learn how to have sex that is free—free from sin, idolatry, guilt, shame, condemnation, death, and separation from God—by having free and frequent marital intimacy. We will study the Song of Songs to learn how to worship God the Creator and enjoy his creation and not worship

brett ullman

his creation (our bodies and their pleasures) as a false god.[98]

Mark Driscoll's teaching series and notes are available on the Mars Hill website, or can be listened to through their app for the iPhone. It's a great series that asks questions like:

- What is your greatest fear in marriage?
- How do you feel when you see your husband pursuing you?
- What does forgiveness look like in your marriage?
- How does your response affect your wife?

These questions are asked to husbands, wives, and singles, demonstrating how important communication is when it comes to marital intimacy. This study also provides personal homework for each person to help them create intimacy through date nights, open lines of communication, and reflect on their marriage and how they view marriage.

In all my research on dating, it seems that almost all relationships you are in up until Grade Eleven don't make it. If we could bet right now with students who are in Grades 7–11 on whether or not their relationships will work, no one in their right mind would make that bet. You may be thinking that your parents met in high school and it worked for them, but that was then and this is now and

---

[98] Mars Hill Church. "The Peasant Princess," http://www.marshillchurch.org/media/the-peasant-princess (February 1, 2011).

chances are it will not work for you. You would never give up your money on a bet that is going to lose 100% of the time, so why are high school students all over the continent willing to give up their sexual purity before giving up their money?

If sexual immorality is your reality, you have many possible outcomes for your life. Two very real possibilities are: pregnancy and STD/STIs (including HIV). That's not to say that your future is set in stone if you practice sexual immorality, but one in four teenage girls now has an STD, and that number is growing.

We have to drive home a message to our girls: sex affects you more than it will your boyfriend. It will always affect you more than a man. You have a greater chance of getting an STD, and the big gamble is pregnancy. Being a single teenage mother in Canada is the single largest factor in determining whether or not you will live below the poverty line for the rest of your life. I'm not trying to use fear tactics when I say that, but that is the reality. Scaring anyone into abstinence and celibacy isn't the way to make this reality known, but knowing the possible and realistic outcomes of sex before marriage is the only way to help young people understand how important a decision it truly is.

I work and speak to thousands of people and I hear a lot of "I wish I had waited," or "I didn't know." But living with a guilty conscious for the rest of your life is not God's way either. We live and serve a forgiving God who is full of grace that redeems us in his eyes. Praying and asking for forgiveness with an earnest heart leads us into the redemptive arms of God. Do some people break out and escape the hardship of single parenting? Sure. But most don't! For that stat to change drastically, it is up to men to step up and take part in raising the kids they leave behind. It also begins with making a similar vow to the one Job makes: *"I made a solemn pact with myself never to undress a girl with my eyes"* (Job 31:1).

Have you seen the commercial for Miller Genuine Draft entitled "Nothing to Hide"? In this commercial, a guy has a girl over to his house for a date and she is searching through his DVD collection, only to come across *Bikini Babes on Mars*. She asks him about the movie only to hear the response, "It's a classic." The reason it's on the shelf with all the other DVDs is that they are all arranged in alphabetical order. She shrugs it off and continues to look through the collection as if to say that is normal.

All students go through media awareness now, and they are all taught that commercials lie—not just some commercials, all commercials. The question becomes what is that lie? If I don't have that car, I won't have the girl. If I don't wear that brand of clothing, I won't look good. I'm too ugly, too fat, too poor. Whatever the commercial is saying, it is a lie. The sad thing about this commercial is that she is saying it's okay (a porn video, alphabetized and out in the open). It's normal, she says. On how many levels is this wrong?

This commercial is telling the lie that:

1) It makes sense to have porn.
2) It makes sense to keep your porn out in the open, etc.

It is about time we make the same kind of decision Job does. Porn is not okay; it is a serious problem that is everywhere in our culture. Once again, where is your line? What do you view as okay or acceptable when it comes to porn? We use porn in everyday language, even inside the church world. One of the big sayings on Facebook is "porno boobs." There are tons of photos out there and all we comment on are boobs.

Also, what have you called sexy today? The fact is that many of the photos put up on Facebook look like they have come right out of a porn photo shoot. Have you noticed how stripper poles have appeared in many different media sources? You can buy exercise programs centered around pole dancing. They are on Brooke Hogan's TV show regularly, as well as in Paris Hilton's photo shoots. Is that where your line is? Is it okay to exercise in a porn atmosphere while watching a porno is completely out of the question?

A 2008 survey by www.xxxchurch.com stated that the average age anyone is introduced to Internet pornography is eleven. That same eleven-year-old child cannot get into a theatre on their own to see *Twilight*, *Robin Hood*, or *Iron Man 2*, yet many of them have had, or can gain access to, Internet porn. There are approximately 420 million pornographic webpages online, making up over 12% of the total amount of websites available. Worldwide porn revenue exceeds 96 billion dollars, which is more money than the revenues of every major league sport combined.

The normalization line, which measures the acceptance of pornography in mainstream culture, is also on the rise. Porn is everywhere and it is up to us to make a decision about how we handle it.

> Our culture is becoming increasingly sexualized and it has taken forty years to go from one dirty magazine under the counter at the local convenience store to today where it is expected that junior high boys have at least one nude shot of their junior high girlfriend on their cell phone.[99]

Where have you drawn your line?

Porn has crossed many lines in popular culture and has become more and more visible on daytime TV. Jenna Jameson was on Oprah on November 19, 2009. Why is this a big deal, you may be asking? When the biggest porn star in the world is on Oprah, times have changed. Porn used to be found in brown paper bags or on the top shelf of the convenience store. But now the biggest porn star ever is featured on one of the most popular shows ever. That is why it is such a big deal.

Porn has become a normal and acceptable part of our culture and worldview. On the program, Jameson kept saying no regrets, no regrets, and no regrets. She said, "I don't know what I am going to tell my kids." She cried as

---

[99] Driscoll, Mark. *Porn-Again Christian: A Frank Discussion on Pornography & Masturbation* (Mars Hill, NC: Mars Hill Church, 2009), p. 15.

she said this, but the thing is, you can't say there are no regrets and then wonder what you are going to tell your kids. God tells us how to escape this type of regret. *"So here's what I want you to do, God helping you: Take your everyday, ordinary life—your sleeping, eating, going-to-work, and walking-around life—and place it before God as an offering"* (Romans 12:1).

Where does lusting fit into this type of life?

It doesn't!

God many times speaks out against whoring our bodies, as he calls it.

> At the head of every street you built your lofty place and made your beauty an abomination, offering yourself to any passerby and multiplying your whoring. You also played the whore with the Egyptians, your lustful neighbors, multiplying your whoring, to provoke me to anger. Behold, therefore, I stretched out my hand against you and diminished your allotted portion and delivered you to the greed of your enemies, the daughters of the Philistines, who were ashamed of your lewd behaviour. (Ezekiel 16:25–27, ESV)

How about the words in Ezekiel 23:18–21?

> When she carried on her whoring so openly and flaunted her nakedness, I turned in disgust from her, as I had turned in disgust from her sister. Yet she increased her whoring, remembering the days of her youth, when she played the whore in the land of Egypt and lusted after her paramours

there, whose members were like those of
donkeys, and whose issue was like that of horses.
Thus you longed for the lewdness of your youth,
when the Egyptians handled your bosom and
pressed your young breasts. (ESV)

The fact is, God spoke boldly about sexual immorality
and was aware that it was a big problem. If God can address
the issue, why can't we? Lust has become such a huge
influence in culture for teens and young adults that it has
begun to affect their future.

About one-third of college men today describe
difficulty achieving and maintaining erections,
which is a stunning figure. Thirty years ago it
would have been way less, more like 5%. I think
the major reason is that if a boy's primary sexual
activity has been masturbating to pornography,
he's going to find it harder to achieve an erection
with an actual girl who's not wearing lingerie,
who's talking...[100]

If we think about that quote in terms of marriages, then
one-third of newly married couples are entering marriage
with a huge problem. Sex is a part of marriage, but what
will happen to these newly married couples? Porn is a huge
deal for everybody today. This needs to be a conversation
that's championed by the church and its leaders, so that they
can help build and maintain the marriages they perform.

[100] Fillion, Kate. "How to Fix Boys," *Macleans Magazine*, January 9, 2008,
http://www.macleans.ca/culture/entertainment/article.jsp?content=2008010
9_70985_70985 (accessed August 10, 2010).

I get ten emails from women who are dealing with porn addiction for every one I receive from a man. That's because men don't want to deal with it, but women are dealing with it everyday. It's about time we challenged each other and held each other accountable to what we're putting in our lives.

There is not one guy reading this book who doesn't struggle with pornography and lust on some level. If they say they're not, they're lying. Just like God speaking to Israel in Ezekiel, we need to be honest with ourselves about the severity of the unholy desires in our lives.

Just like God speaking to Israel in Ezekiel, we need to be honest with ourselves about the severity of unholy desires in our lives.

How can we fix the problem?

Accountability software. I run Covenant Eyes (www.covenanteyes.com) and X3WATCH (www.x3-watch.com). I can go home tonight and go onto any porn site I want, but tomorrow I will have two guys calling me, asking, "What's up?" There is nothing more frightening than having your personal life under a microscope by those closest to you, but that accountability, if you're honest about moving past an addiction, is the only way to succeed.

Here are some helpful resources that deal with issues surrounding pornography:

- Accountability software.
    o www.x3watch.com
    o www.covenanteyes.com
    o www.safeeyes.com

- *The Dirty Little Secret*, by Craig Gross (Grand Rapids, MI: Zondervan, 2006)
- www.xxxchurch.com
- *Pure Eyes*, by Craig Gross (Grand Rapids, MI: Baker Books, 2010)
- *Pure Heart*, by Craig Gross (Grand Rapids, MI: Baker Books, 2010)
- *The Struggle: Let's Be Honest, Every Guy Struggles with It*, by Steve Gerali (Colorado Springs, CO: NavPress, 2003)
- *Every Men's Battle (Married Men)*, by Stephen Arterburn (Colorado Springs, CO: Waterbrook Press, 2000)
- *Every Women's Battle (Married Women)*, by Stephen Arterburn (Colorado Springs, CO: Waterbrook Press, 2003)
- *Every Young Man's Battle (Adolescent Males)*, by Stephen Arterburn (Colorado Springs, CO: Waterbrook Press, 2002)
- *Every Young Woman's Battle (Adolescent Females)*, by Stephen Arterburn (Colorado Springs, CO: Waterbrook Press, 2004)
- *Preparing Your Son for Every Man's Battle: Honest Conversations About Sexual Integrity (Parents to Son)*, by Stephen Arterburn (Colorado Springs, CO: Waterbrook Press, 2010)
- *When Young Men are Tempted: Sexual Purity for Guys in the Real World (Youth)*, by Bill Perkins

and Randy Southern (Grand Rapids, MI: Zondervan, 2007)

- *Forbidden Fruit (Youth),* by Mark D. Regnerus (Oxford, NY: Oxford University Press, 2007)
- *Sex Has a Price Tag: Discussions About Sexuality, Spirituality and Self-Respect,* by Pam Stenzel and Crystal Kirgiss (Grand Rapids, MI: Zondervan, 2003)

For more information about these resources, and many others, check out the Worlds Apart website.[101]

In the fall of 2008, the Parent Factor did a huge study on teen sex called The Backgrounder. The study talks about three factors which contribute to having a successful, protective parenting influence in the home. The first is having an intact family structure.

> "Perhaps the most profound change in the American family over the past four decades has been the decline in the share of children growing up in households with both biological parents." In 1960, 88 percent of all children lived with two parents, compared to 68 percent in 2007. In 1960, 5 percent of all children born were to unmarried mothers. That figure rose to 38.5 percent in 2006. Thus, policies and programs that bolster the intact family structure and

---

[101] http://www.worldsapart.org/christian-support/sensitive-issues-hot-topics/sexuality-a-pornography.html

promote healthy marriages may reduce teen
sexual activity.[102]

Yes, every man struggles with pornography, but Craig
Gross says in his new book that about sixty percent of
Christian women struggle as well:

> 60% of churchgoing females admitted to having
> significant struggles with lust. 40% admitted to
> being involved in sexual sin in the past year. 20%
> struggle with looking at pornography on an
> ongoing basis.[103]

The pornography question goes far beyond just the men
in our church and the boys in our youth groups; we also
have to start addressing the appalling silence in regards to
helping mothers and daughters through this battle.

We want to protect our marriages for the sake of our
kids. Parents also need to express their disapproval of oral
sex. We need to have these conversations with our kids,
telling them that oral sex is not acceptable. Have you ever
had those weird talks with parents when they look at you
and ask if they really have to say that to their kids? When
that happens to me, all I want to respond with is, "Yes,
grow up and be a parent. You're forty years old. You say
should be able to say 'oral sex' to your kid."

> Mixed messages could potentially diminish any
> positive effects parental values have on delaying

[102] Kim, Christine C. "Teen Sex: The Parent Factor," *The Heritage Foundation*,
Backgrounder, October 7, 2008, p. 4.
[103] Gross, Craig. *Eyes of Integrity* (Grand Rapids, MI: Baker Books, 2010), p. 30.

teen sexual behavior. In a national poll, teens were asked: "Suppose a parent or other adult tells you/a teen the following: 'Don't have sex, but if you do you should use birth control for protection.' Do you think this is a message that encourages you/teens to have sex?" One teen in two responded affirmatively, indicating that, to many teens, a qualified "no" translates into a perceived "yes."[104]

Our kids need to hear that from us.

The last factor is having a strong-parent child relationship.

Parent-child relationship quality or connectedness is often measured by the level of satisfaction teens and their parents experience in their relationships with one another; the amount of warmth, love, affection, and communication teens report receiving from their parents; and the level of parental involvement in their children's lives.[105]

Some of the parenting books I've read fall on either of those extremes. They say that you are either a parent or a friend, when in actuality you are both. You cannot be one or the other; you need to create a balance. The Backgrounder sets up what we can do as parents to have the best influence on our children's perception of sex.

[104] Kim, Christine C. "Teen Sex: The Parent Factor," *The Heritage Foundation*, Backgrounder, October 7, 2008, p. 6.
[105] Ibid.

The two strongest links appear to be parental values regarding teen sex and parents' relationships with their children. Consequently, parents should:

- Avoid sending ambiguous and mixed messages about teen sex;
- Convey clearly to their teens their values on this subject;
- Focus on imparting clearly defined values— simply discussing sex, contraceptives, and physiology does not necessarily protect teens; and
- Seek to strengthen their relationships with their teenage children.[106]

You have to enjoy each other enough in a friendship before you can speak truth into your children's lives. Mark Driscoll, in one of his podcasts, says that we should ask, "When was the last time you enjoyed your family?" That's a question I ask myself constantly. I actually paused the podcast for a moment and thought about how much time we spend with our families. But more importantly, when was the last time we *enjoyed* our time with our families?

Here are some helpful resources for issues dealing with marriage, parenthood, and adulthood:

- *The Peasant Princess* study, available on the Mars Hill website

[106] Ibid., p. 9.

(http://www.marshillchurch.org/media/the-peasant-princess)

- *Parenting Beyond Your Capacity*, by Reggie Joiner and Carey Nieuwhof (Colorado Springs, CO: David C. Cook, 2010)
- *Revolutionary Parenting*, by George Barna (Carol Stream, IL: Barna Books, 2007)
- *Nurturing the Heart of Marriage*, a CD by Dr. Merry C. Lin (http://www.drlinandassociates.com)
- *Fatherless Generation*, by John Sowers (Grand Rapids, MI: Zondervan, 2010)
- *Every Man's Marriage*, by Stephen Arterburn (Waterville, ME: Walker Large Print, 2002)
- *Every Women's Marriage*, by Stephen Arterburn (Colorado Springs, CO: Waterbrook Press, 2006)

Self-Injury

There is no issue in our world today that brings up more emotional feelings than the issue of self-harm. Henri Nouwen, one of my favourite authors, says, "Our life is full of brokenness... How can we live with that brokenness without becoming bitter and resentful except by returning again and again to God's faithful presence in our lives?"[107] I am a Christian and a follower of the way. Do I believe God can heal? Yes, I do.

---

[107] Nouwen, Henri. *Sabbatical Journey: The Diary of His Final Year* (New York, NY: Crossroad Publishers, 1998), p. 134.

Do you?

Do I believe God is there, in our healing? Yes.

Again, do you?

I will, however, part ways with the faith questions for a moment, because this is what I hear all the time: "Brett, I talked to my pastor, I talked to my youth leader, I talked to my whoever, and I told them I am struggling with cutting and their response was to pray to Jesus and you will be fine." Then they leave the room.

I will acknowledge that God can heal, but let me say this: that answer, to me, is religious abuse. We are called to be the hands and feet of God.

> The way God designed our bodies is a model for understanding our lives together as a church: every part dependent on every other part, the parts we mention and the parts we don't, the parts we see and the parts we don't. If one part hurts, every other part is involved in the hurt, and in the healing. If one part flourishes, every other part enters into the exuberance. (1 Corinthians 12:24–26)

If you or someone you know is hurting because they cut or harm one another, and you have heard this, I am sorry. All of us are called to be people who stand beside each other, care for each other, and help heal one another. But we don't. We walk away, over and over again.

So yes, I acknowledge my faith, but how do we be the hands and feet of God?

Personally, I explain self-injury as hurting yourself in any way, shape, or form, with anything you could ever imagine, to get beyond overwhelming feelings and emotions.

A man actually yelled out at one of my talks, outright yelled from the crowd, "Why would you ever talk about this?"

I flipped my slide and he quietly sat back down in his seat.

In 2008, *The Globe and Mail* published results from a Canadian study finding that one in six teens are injuring themselves through the act of self-harming.[108] Most of us who speak on, or in the field of, helping kids who self-harm would place it more in the range of one in five. The man who yelled at me saw these same stats. This is a growing issue that needs to be addressed because people who are unfamiliar with self-harm and why it is happening have a very skewed opinion on the subject.

One of the first things I hear when I talk about this subject with teens is, "Yeah, I know that kid. They're emo." If you think the only person who struggles with self-harm wears black more than someone else, you are just wrong. There is no "that" person, there is no nationality, there is no ethnicity and age... it does not matter, because anyone can struggle with self-injury. The youngest person I have dealt with is in Grade Three and the oldest is a

---

[108] Picard, André. "One in six teens inflict self-harm." *Globe and Mail,* January 29, 2010, http://www.theglobeandmail.com/life/article663414.ece (accessed on July 10, 2010).

seventy-seven-year-old. Self-injury does not pick and choose based on anything.

Last year, at an event called Creation, I was speaking on the main stage and announced that I would be speaking during a breakout session later that day on self-injury and if anyone wanted to know more, they could come by. At least three people said to me after my main stage talk that no one would show up for a breakout on self-injury. It is funny how things work out. Those three people were all in the front few rows when I spoke to the four to five thousand people who showed up that afternoon. We were in a forest and we could not move. After the talk, I stayed to talk with those who were there and a couple walked up. They said that they had been about to leave when the husband turned to his wife.

"Honey, I cut," he said.

She went on to tell me that she ripped into him, thinking he was joking and kidding around after my talk. But then she noticed the tears.

"Brett, I thought people who cut were Goth, wore black all the time, or they were people who wear long sleeve shirts in the summer. Brett, I am a fifty-year-old youth pastor. I wear Abercrombie and Fitch. Cutting isn't exclusive, because that is who I am."

Cutting affects so much more than a gender, ethnicity, or cultural subgroup. The reality is that even as you are reading this book there will be people who acknowledge for the very first time that they self-injure. They will admit to themselves that they no longer want to live that way and no longer want to live in silence. How can I be so sure of that, you ask? The answer is quite simple. There are a lot of people hurting in silence and many who struggle with self-harm every day. When I am away speaking, there are usually a few people in the crowd who will come up and acknowledge the fact that they are cutting, or hurting themselves in other ways.

There is no particular look for someone who struggles with cutting. Notice that I did not say a "cutter"—I hate labels. If you deal with cutting and you are reading this book, note that you are not a "cutter." It is your struggle. You can and will get beyond it. It is not your identity. It is not who you are. It is not the only thing you are about.

I once read the following statement: "You are infinitely more rich than any single label might say."

Self-injury can include eating disorders like anorexia, bulimia, and binge eating. Self-injury can include cutting. This is the conversation for today. Self-injury is suicide and this is a conversation I have with people on an ongoing basis.

Disney star Demi Lovato is one of many celebrities who have admitted to suffering through issues with self-harm in one form or another. She entered a rehab facility in 2010 so that she could find a safe place to deal with her lifelong battle with eating disorders.

> But I will deal with it for the rest of my life because it is a life-long disease. I don't think there's going to be a day when I don't think about food or my body, but I'm living with it, and

> I wish I could tell young girls to find their safe
> place and stay with it.[109]

Here is a talented and beautiful girl who has dealt with bullying, which led to hurting. She had no clear outlet for her feelings. Her message is to find a safe place for that outlet, so that the emotions and hurt don't build up and lead to self-injury.

> It's very crucial that you get your feelings out—
> but don't ever inflict harm on your own body
> because your body is so sacred.[110]

We're in a position of authority in our kids' lives. It's our responsibility to allow them to feel safe enough to share their feelings with someone who shows genuine care and regard for how they feel. If we're not providing a safe place, their emotions build and they will look for another outlet. The danger is when that outlet becomes self-injury, a release of emotional pain through bodily harm.

Demi Lovato isn't the only celebrity to deal with this issue. Portia de Rossi, in her book *Unbearable Lightness: A Story of Loss and Gain*, goes into her battle with eating disorders and how she deals with it everyday. Angelina Jolie, Johnny Depp, and Amy Winehouse have also spoken out on how self-injury has affected their lives.

---

[109] Radar. "Demi Lovato On Her Eating Disorder: 'It's a Life-Long Disease,'" www.radaronline.com/exclusives/2011/04/demi-lovato-her-eating-disorder-its-a-life-long-disease (accessed: April 13, 2011).
[110] Ibid.

Self-injury doesn't just affect one group of people; it can affect anyone, because it relies on emotion and how an individual releases those emotions.

I get calls like this from the very schools our kids attend. Someone from the school might say, "Brett, we just had a Grade Four kid hang himself. Can you come and speak to the students?"

First off, what kind of world are we living in when we have Grade Four students who do not want to be a part of it any longer? My response is always the same: "No, I can't."

I am not a crisis team and this book won't have all the answers, because I am not a counsellor. In reality, there is no speaker in the world who can walk in and make things okay... because things are not okay. If you are reading this book and are thinking about suicide, or you struggle with self-injury, please contact a counsellor, or visit www.yourstory.info.

When I talk about drugs and alcohol, I am not talking about addiction. We are talking about people who do these things to get beyond something in their lives. We are talking about that bad day that happens from time to time, and let's be honest—six beers work. I am not saying it's okay to go and drink six beers if you have a bad day; I am saying that when drugs and alcohol are used in that way, it is an escape from something we see no end to.

We know there is hope on the outside. People say they live in this dark hole in their head and they just don't know how to get out. Maybe you feel like Job when he is talking to God about his life. Here is a guy who could really go for those six beers to escape his broken spirit.

> My spirit is broken,
> my days used up,
> my grave dug and waiting.
> See how these mockers close in on me?
> How long do I have to put up with their
>   insolence?
>
> O God, pledge your support for me.
> Give it to me in writing, with your signature.
> You're the only one who can do it!
> These people are so useless!
> You know firsthand how stupid they can be.
> You wouldn't let them have the last word, would
>   you?
> Those who betray their own friends
> leave a legacy of abuse to their children.
>
> God, you've made me the talk of the town—
> people spit in my face;
> I can hardly see from crying so much;
> I'm nothing but skin and bones.
> Decent people can't believe what they're seeing;
> the good-hearted wake up and insist I've given
>   up on God.
>
> But principled people hold tight, keep a firm
>   grip on life,
> sure that their clean, pure hands will get stronger
>   and stronger!

Maybe you'd all like to start over,
to try it again, the bunch of you.
So far I haven't come across one scrap
of wisdom in anything you've said.
My life's about over. All my plans are smashed,
all my hopes are snuffed out—
My hope that night would turn into day,
my hope that dawn was about to break.
If all I have to look forward to is a home in the
       graveyard,
if my only hope for comfort is a well-built coffin,
If a family reunion means going six feet under,
and the only family that shows up is worms,
Do you call that hope?
Who on earth could find any hope in that?
No. If hope and I are to be buried together,
I suppose you'll all come to the double funeral!
(Job 17)

God goes on to tell Job that he is the hope Job needs. This is quite a funny conversation between God and Job because God presents Job with a situation that is impossible to accomplish on his own. God asks Job, *"Or can you pull in the sea beast, Leviathan, with a fly rod and stuff him in your creel?"* (Job 41:1) Basically, can you go out on a boat and catch the Lock Ness Monster with a fishing pole? God again asks Job, *"What hope would you have with such a creature? Why, one look at him would do you in!"* (Job 41:9)

Is this not how we feel when we look into the black hole we think we are living in? Do we really think we can get past our own situations? God is essentially saying, "If you can't hold your own against my glowering visage, how then do you expect to stand up to me? Who can confront me and get away with it? I'm in charge of all this—I run this universe!" Do we take our bad days and turn them into a Leviathan? Do we think the only way to get beyond our struggles is drugs and alcohol? If so, the question becomes, where are you putting your hope?

Is it in God or in drugs?

The Bible speaks about hope over and over again. 1 Thessalonians 5:6–11 encourages us to place our hope in each other, our faith, and in God.

> So let's not sleepwalk through life like those others. Let's keep our eyes open and be smart. People sleep at night and get drunk at night. But not us! Since we're creatures of Day, let's act like it. Walk out into the daylight sober, dressed up in faith, love, and the hope of salvation. God didn't set us up for an angry rejection but for salvation by our Master, Jesus Christ. He died for us, a death that triggered life. Whether we're awake with the living or asleep with the dead, we're alive with him! So speak encouraging words to one another. Build up hope so you'll all be together in this, no one left out, no one left behind. I know you're already doing this; just keep on doing it.

I want you to read a poem that was posted on my Your Story page (www.yourstory.info). This poem addresses the very question we have been looking at above—where are you putting your hope?

Only His Blood can heal our wounds. How did it come to this, how did my eyes not see? How can I be waking up with scars and bruises instead of joy and life? When did the dark begin to override the light, and will the light come back? I believed you. You told me and I believed you. And now I am here, bruised and scarred, with only the words resonating in my mind (only His blood can heal our wounds, only His blood can heal our wounds). Oh please, take it back, take me back, make me beautiful. Make my scars a memory that doesn't burn, and make these bruises the verdict of what was, not what is. I believed you. You told me and I believed you. I want to be whole again. I want to breathe again. I want to live again. I want to wake up tomorrow and these bruises be gone, and these scars never come back. I am better than this (only His blood can heal our wounds, only His blood can heal our wounds). You promised me beauty for ashes, beauty for ashes. Take these ashes and make them beautiful. They are burnt and bloody and dry, but I know you can make them beautiful. These ashes are the sin that ate at me, convinced me, lied to me, told me these bruises I deserved. I believed you. You told me and I believed you. Make the ashes beautiful (only His blood can heal our wounds, only His blood can heal our wounds). This is the final show. This is the last day I wake up like this. Today I will wear my bruises and scars as a sign, that tomorrow the light will come back... and His blood will heal my wounds...[111]

---

[111] Anonymous, "His Blood," *Your Story*,

Where is your hope? Is it in things that can drag us back down, or is it in the blood that can wash us clean?

There are two types of people who are reading this book, and even more accurately there are two types of people in the world—

- Those who self-injure, and
- Those who know someone who self-injures.

When I speak at your schools and ask the group if they know anyone who struggles with eating disorders, cutting, drugs, etc., the whole room puts up their hands. We all know someone who struggles, but how do we respond to that person? Is it with religious abuse, or with a message of hope?

How many people do you know who struggle with self-injury in any form?

In her book *Cut,* Patricia McCormick says this, "There are all kinds of things in the world you could use to hurt yourself. All kinds of things you could turn into weapons. Even if you wanted to give them all to me, it would be impossible... I can't keep you safe, only you can."[112] If you are reading this today and you are that person, realize that you are the only person who can stop. No pastor, no teacher, no person can tell you to stop; it has to be you, when you come to a place where you can say, "This doesn't work." Out of five thousand emails I have received from those who self-injure, not one of them ever says it is

---

http://www.yourstory.info/content/view/132/12/ (accessed August 5, 2010).
[112] McCormick, Patricia. *Cut* (Asherville, NC: Front Street, 2000), p. 126.

an easy way to cope. Instead, all they say is that it's the only way they know how to cope.

Is that you?

Is self-injury the only way you know how to cope with a bad day, bad relationship, bad grades, or anything else that has gone wrong recently? It has to be you. Karen Conterio, in her book *Bodily Harm*, says this: "There is nobody on earth who can, or will, save you from yourself. You are going to have to do it for yourself—but not by yourself."[113] That means family or friends are not the ones to make you stop. But like in the passage from 1 Thessalonians, they can give you the support you need. Stopping has to be a conscious decision of your own. It won't be easy, but it comes down to where you see hope coming from and who can speak hope into your life. The problem is that we struggle with speaking hope and encouragement into the lives of our friends who are dealing with self-injury.

As parents, we need to start asking our kids how they are doing. I don't mean the casual surface question you ask every night after school: "How was your day?" I mean the heartfelt questions that penetrate our kids' hurts and expose their true feelings.

In late 2010, a young girl took her life, bringing to light the fact that although her parents had had the drug talk and the sex talk, they hadn't addressed the subject of mental health.

[113] Conterio, Karen, Wendy Lader, and Jennifer Kingson Bloom. *Bodily Harm: The Breakthrough Treatment Program for Self-Injurers* (New York, NY: Hyperion, 1998), p. x.

> I wish we did talk about it before, but we just
> didn't think it was there, maybe because... [she]
> didn't let us know that there were some deeper
> issues that were inside of her.[114]

Feelings of loneliness and desperation, when it comes to teen depression and suicide, can be the most difficult to deal with as parents because of the fact that our kids don't want to share these issues with anyone, including their friends.

Here are some warning sings to look for at home in regards to depression and suicide from Royal Ottawa:

- Withdrawal from family and friends, part-time jobs, and a loss of interest in items that were previously enjoyed.
- Slipping grades and skipped classes, or problems concentrating.
- Reckless behaviour.
- New or increased self-harm behaviour.
- Increased aggression and conflicts with others.
- Giving away their favourite possessions.
- Expressing feelings of depression, hopelessness, and helplessness.
- Changes in eating, sleeping, and personal hygiene habits.

---

[114] CTV. *Ottawa*. 25 Feb 2011. 4 Apr. 2011
<http://ottawa.ctv.ca/servlet/an/local/CTVNews/20110225/OTT_Daron_1102
25/20110225/?hub=OttawaHome>.

- Frequent complaints about physical symptoms often related to emotions, such as stomach aches, headaches, and fatigue.
- Talk of death or suicide. This could include jokes about suicide.[115]

Just as important as being aware of the warning signs of suicide and depression are the reactions and conversations we have with our kids. The way we react to their feelings needs to convey the seriousness of their feelings, but also the love and concern we have for their safety. Royal Ottawa also has a section on their page about how to talk to your child about suicide. Here are some of their strategies:

- Listen without judgment and with an open mind.
- Don't dismiss their stress or feelings of loss.
- Show and communicate acceptance towards their feelings. Their feelings need to be acknowledged.
- Let them know that they matter to you and that you will support them in any way they need.
- Ask about suicide directly if you are concerned it may be an issue. "Are you thinking about suicide?" They do not become more suicidal if they are asked about it.[116]

---

[115] Royal Ottawa: Mental Health Centre. "Information for Parents," http://static.capitaltickets.ca/sens_foundation/documents/30153.SuicideHandoutParent.pdf (accessed: April 5, 2011).
[116] Ibid.

So get help and take threats seriously.

I hear this all the time: "Brett, I was at this party and a girl pulled up her sleeve and she hurts herself."

"What did you do?" I ask.

"I got uncomfortable and went home."

Are we as parents doing the same things to our children by not actively engaging them on the issues of depression and suicide? Do we know the warning signs? We need to make sure that our youth groups are safe places for those who are struggling with these issues.

I once received the following anonymous email in regards to how a person who self-injures felt about their safety within their own group:

> If my church knew I cut, burned, scratched or anything of the sort, I would be removed from ministry so fast I wouldn't be able to blink. The one place I love and long to be involved in would be taken away, even with the best intentions, and I can't let that happen. Thus, I live a life of secrets. I help the youth as best I can but tell very little of where I've come from or why I don't date.

Imagine if that person felt accepted and cared for enough to share their story. Imagine how many future lives they could speak into if they felt their life would not come crashing down around them once they were honest about their own struggles.

Within each of our youth ministries, there will be someone who struggles with self-harm. We need to allow the process of healing to be one of acceptance and care, and not one of judgment. Why are we not addressing these issues at home and in our churches? Are we afraid of the life-changing conversations that will need to happen afterwards? Are we unwilling to walk through life with the very same kids we were walking with before they told us about the self-injury in their lives?

Does our own security come before their insecurity?

If so, I will give you the same line my professor gave me during my studies in the Arrow Leadership[117] program: "Suck it up, princess." That is my response. Instead of walking away from someone in need, suck up your pride, suck up your ego, and grow up. I say that to everyone, whether you are four, forty-four, or a hundred and four. It does not matter what age you are. We all need to grow up and look in the mirror in search of the caring human being God calls us to be in Matthew 22.

How can we love our neighbour if we are not willing to stick it out with them through the tough times? If someone in need approaches us and our response is to go away, what message does that send to the person looking for help? Is this promoting our ancient faith worldview? Was that Jesus' response to those who came to him in need? Was that the attitude Jesus took to the cross? Stand your ground, especially if you are a Christian. Explain that you might not understand what they are going through, or even understand their need to harm themselves, but that you will be there for them. We need to start letting people know that we will work through it with them. We need to be

---

[117] www.arrowleadership.org

willing to go see counsellors with them if that is what they want, or to be available as accountability partners. We need to be there for them as they say, "I am lost and don't know what to do."

Most people who come out of a life of self-injury usually note one person, one person who never left their side. Marv Penner, in his book *Hope and Healing for Kids Who Cut*, challenges us to be available to be that one person in the life of a young person who entrusts his or her story to you.[118] We can be that person. We just need to be in the same room as them. I challenge you to start having real conversations with the people you go to school with. Stop having the whole "How are you... fine... good" conversations and start seriously having "No, how are you really?" conversations. That's the only way to start promoting healing and hope to those around us.

Actions are the things we do. Our actions can be forms of self-injury, and I would include promiscuous sex as self-injury. Erwin McManus, the pastor of Mosaic, a church in Los Angeles, says, "Fake intimacy is better than wide open loneliness." I know a lot of teens and young adults who just fall into bed with someone thinking they will find some great closeness or compassion, but all they find is pain, guilt, and more sorrow. But our actions arise from our feelings. The single largest feeling in your generation is the feeling of abandonment, not love, not compassion, not joy— but abandonment.

What do you feel abandoned from?

---

[118] Penner, Marv. *Hope and Healing for Kids Who Cut: The Diary of His Final Year* (Grand Rapids, MI: Zondervan, 2008), p. 26.

Our feelings come from something deep, though, and they are our stories, our histories, and we all have them. Some of them are easy to deal with, right? We didn't make the basketball team or we got fired or we failed the test... we can deal with those stories. There are some things, though, that we are just not able to handle.

A girl in Grade Nine once said to me, "Brett, I think I know why I cut and am bulimic."

"Why?"

"Well, my mom left my dad."

"I'm sorry."

"I came home the next day and found my dad hanging in our garage."

Another girl told me this about why she struggles with every form of self-injury I have named: "I go to Western University and I was raped on my first date."

So, what do I mean by dealing with stories? Last year, I had to deal with some things. I had three important people I love pass away in less than a year. My Uncle Bob died of a heart attack, my Aunt Gail lost her life to breast cancer, and the one that rocked me was the death of one of my best friends, Warren Parker. Each death was painful to deal with on their own, but when you add in the pain and feelings of losing multiple people, it became almost unbearable.

Warren's death was a surprise because of the nature in which it happened. A drunk driver killed him. I was the best man at his wedding and it was one of those moments when you just start to fall apart. After each loss, I started to have this feeling of incredible sadness and unbelievable anger weaved together to form this weird new feeling. All I wanted to do was get beyond it. Honestly, six beers would have helped anyone get beyond it, but for how long? Maybe an hour, one hour of freedom, but then an hour later you're back in the same place with the same anger, the same sadness, never dealing with the issue.

How do we deal?

We deal by sitting down with a counsellor. It was fascinating to me that wherever I went after Warren's death, everyone I met on every flight I went on seemed to be a counsellor. This went on for a couple of months. I would have these conversations over and over.

"What do you do?"

"I am a counsellor."

"Really?"

I mean, come on, this was like the fifth counsellor I sat beside. I began to have conversations with people I didn't even know who helped me walk through this conversation.

ACTIONS

⬆

FEELINGS

⬆

YOUR STORY

The steps looked something like this:

First, deal with your root issue. So many of us have deep hurts at our core that we have never addressed. We need to deal with them before we can move forward. Secondly, we need to learn how to deal with our feelings. I know that when I have a bad day, I watch TV. It helps me relax and I can lose myself for a couple of moments in my favourite shows. What I do is different from what my wife does, which is different from what you will need to do. We all do different things to deal with our feelings. Learn what works best for you. Try writing down ten actions that help you deal with your feelings. Maybe it is reading, writing, or drawing. It could be watching TV, listening to the soothing voice of Frank Sinatra... it could be just about anything.

EXAMPLE: WATCH TV
1.
2.
3.
4.
5.
6.

7.
8.
9.
10.

Here are some helpful resources dealing with self-injury:

- www.yourstory.info
- *Hope and Healing for Kids Who Cut*, by Marv Penner (Grand Rapids, MI: Zondervan, 2008)
- *The Wounding Embrace*, a DVD by Brett Ullman (www.brettullman.com)
- *Inside A Cutter's Mind: Understanding and Helping Those who Self-Injure*, by Jerusha Clark and Dr. Earl Henslin (Colorado Springs, CO: Think, 2007)
- *Help! My Kids Are Hurting: A Survival Guide to Working with Students in Pain*, by Marv Penner (Grand Rapids, MI: Zondervan, 2005)
- *Your Secret Name*, by Kary Oberbrunner (Grand Rapids, MI: Zondervan, 2010)
- *Rid of My Disgrace: Hope and Healing for Victims of Sexual Assault*, by Justin S. Holcomb and Lindsey A. Holcomb (Wheaton, IL: Crossway, 2011)

- *Cutting: Understanding and Overcoming Self-Mutilation*, by Steven Levenkron (New York, NY: W.W. Northon, 2006)

Kill Zones: Violence in Media

The first video game in the first-person shooter craze was not *007: Golden Eye* for the Nintendo 64 game console. It was actually Atari's *Battlezone*, and it was released in 1980. Then they made *Phantom Slayer*, and they said they had made the first-person shooter scary. Really, it's just a clear head that moves around. It all started to change after that, but first we had *Duke Nukem*. Essentially it was just Mario with a blond haircut. I don't care what they say, he was a Mario clone.

Doom, to me, is when everything changed. Now we could kill without a gun because we had a chainsaw that could cut off people's faces. In the two years after it was first released in 1993, it is estimated that ten million people downloaded the game. Every single first-person shooter after that is considered a clone of what *Doom* started.

Mike Gummelt from Raven Software said, "We'd have to really be either extremely stubborn, in deep denial, or lying to say that the violence in our games doesn't affect people."[119] In the same breath, he also mentions that games like *Doom* are only the beginning of the problem. "But I don't think it's *Doom* that's the problem, it's the free

---

[119] Brown, Janelle. "Doom, Quake and mass murder," *Salon*, April 23, 1999, http://www.salon.com/technology/feature/1999/04/23/gamers (accessed August 4, 2010).

proliferation and general acceptance of violence in our society. In movies, on TV and (to a lesser degree due to limits of realism) in games. That kind of widespread violence and cruelty in media definitely takes the shock out of violence and gore."[120] *The New York Times* describes the games as "games in which players stalk their opponents through dungeon-like environments and try to kill them with high-powered weapons."[121] It is about time we begin to ask ourselves what games like *Doom* are teaching us. What are they saying is normal, and what do they promote as normal?

We have to begin to ask ourselves, why do we need to live out scenarios where killing is considered a right response, or the way to gain more points? The Bible says, *"You shall not murder"* (Exodus 20:13, NIV). Technically speaking, stepping on a mushroom in Mario Bros. is considered killing, but I think we can all agree there is a huge difference between stepping on a mushroom and decapitating a body for the thrill of it.

Tom Bissell, in *Extra Lives*, explains the point where killing in first-person shooters becomes alarming.

> I do not mind being asked to kill in the shooter: Killing is part of the contract. What I do mind is not feeling anything in particular—not even a numbness—after having killed in such numbers. Many shooters ask the gamer to use violence

[120] Ibid.
[121] Johnson, Dirk and James Brooke. "Portrait of Outcasts Seeking to Stand Out From Other Groups," *The New York Times*, April 22, 1999, http://www.nytimes.com/library/national/042299colo-school-suspects.html (accessed August 4, 2010).

> against pure, ambiguous evil: monsters, Nazis, corporate goons, aliens of Ottoman territorial ambition. Yet these shooters typically have nothing to say about evil and violence, other than that evil is evil and violent is violent.[122]

However, in Matthew 5:21–22 we are told that hate and anger are just as bad as murder: *"You have heard that it was said to the people long ago, 'Do not murder, and anyone who murders will be subject to judgment.' But I tell you that anyone who is angry with his brother will be subject to judgment"* (NIV).

Aggressive and excessively violent video games such as *Manhunt* and *Red Dead Redemption* promote worldviews centered on hatred and violence—whereas Mario stepping on a mushroom is not rooted in malice. There needs to be an understanding between what we know is right and what we know is wrong. We know that running through streets, or the Wild West, killing individuals is wrong.

Rockstar Games' newest release *Red Dead Redemption* comes with an M rating—for mature audiences only. It warns the buyer that this game is filled with blood, intense violence, nudity, strong language, strong sexual content, and drug use.[123] The main objective of the game is quite simple and summed up on their official website as: "Red Dead Redemption is an epic battle for survival in a beautiful open world as John Marston struggles to bury his blood-

[122] Bissell, Tom. *Extra Lives: Why Video Games Matter*. New York: Pantheon Books, 2010.134

[123] Rockstar Games, "Info," *Red Dead Redemption*, http://www.rockstargames.com/reddeadredemption/info (accessed August 7, 2010).

stained past, one man at a time."[124] The video game also condones tying up women and placing them on railroad tracks to gain points and also regularly refers to women as b—s and w—s. Rockstar Games has once again pushed the limits on their graphic video games, taking their controversial worldviews from the streets of Vice City to the wide open plains of the 1960s' western frontier.

In 2000, *Soldier of Fortune* was first created with the aid of an ex-army colonel. The game featured twenty-six kill zones on the human body and each victim responded differently depending on which "kill zone" was affected, what weapon was used, and how far away the attacker was. All that information was written into the coding for the game. The creators of *Mortal Kombat* were featured in the Summer 2010 issue of *Electronic Gaming Monthly*, which was entitled *Remaking a Legend*. "Mortal Kombat is known for and associated with violence, and we're definitely going back to that." Ed Boon, who is the creative director, tells us everything we need to know about the video game franchise. This game is all about violence. The developers of this game are actually writing into the code how the body would react if an arm was ripped off. This is so that while you are playing you are driven to the final frontier of video game violence, as the article points out.

Do you really need to know how the body would react if an arm was ripped off, or if a body is cut in half? These video games are actually designed to make you feel for the character. Especially in games like *Far Cry 2, Call of Duty,*

---

[124] Ibid.

and many of the other violent first-person shooters out there.

> The maintained first-person was intended to provide what Hocking calls a psychosomatic "shortcut" to the gamer's brain. "The reason is twofold. First, you create this bond between the player and character. When he has to pull a twig out of his arm, he feels some kind of illusion of pain. Second, all of it was designed to build up to that moment when you're holding your buddy in your arms. It's a huge chain of connectedness that pays off in that moment."[125]

Quentin Tarantino has this problem all the time. He asks himself, *What colour do I make the blood?* Apparently it's a big deal. "I'm really particular about the blood, so we're using a mixture depending on the scenes. I say, 'I don't want horror movie blood, alright? I want Samurai blood.' You can't pour this raspberry pancake syrup on a sword and have it look good. You have to have this special kind of blood that you only see in samurai movies."[126] Have we become so desensitized to blood and violence that we write off movies because the colour of blood was not realistic enough? Quentin seems to think so, as he reshoots entire scenes if the colour is off or the sound is not realistic enough.

---

[125] Bissell, Tom. *Extra Lives: Why Video Games Matter* (New York, NY: Pantheon Books, 2010), p. 149.

[126] Jakes, Susan. "Blood Sport," *Time Magazine*, September 9, 2002, http://www.time.com/time/magazine/article/0,9171,349193,00.html (accessed April 4, 2010).

I don't even think we realize how our minds react to this kind of violence anymore. I do not believe the results of every study that comes out linking violence and behaviour, because for every person who says violence influences you, you can find one who says it does not. However, somewhere there must be a little voice that says this cannot be good; it just cannot be good to expose ourselves constantly to something God tells us to avoid.

First-person shooters aren't going anywhere anytime soon. *Call of Duty: Black Ops* was released on November 9, 2010 and the sales have been unreal. We have not seen numbers like this since the last *Call of Duty* release.

Here is a portion of Activision's press release concerning its worldwide figures.

> *Call of Duty: Black Ops* continues to set sell-through records crossing the $1 billion mark in sales worldwide since its launch in November, according to internal Activision estimates.
> In its first five days alone, the game sold more than $650 million worldwide, outpacing theatrical box office, book and video game sales records for five-day worldwide sell through in dollars, according to internal Activision estimates and boxofficemojo.com. The game exceeded Activision's previous five-day worldwide record of $550 million set by last year's *Call of Duty: Modern Warfare® 2*.
> To date, more than 600 million hours have been logged playing *Call of Duty: Black Ops* since the game launched on November 9, 2010. According to Microsoft, the average player logs

on more than once a day and plays for more
than one hour each time. Over half of that time is
spent playing online with and against friends,
illustrating the unique social characteristics of the
game.[127]

First-person shooters are taking violence and turning it
into a social gathering. Now we can log on and kill with
each other. Not only are video game companies making it a
social activity with multi-player online options, but the
challenge is always how to make the game better. In order
to make it better, the only logical thing to do is enhance a
game's killing options, right?

Here's one review I read:

This is probably the most brutal COD so far.
Forget slashing knife kills: here they're brutal,
hacking attacks on struggling foes. It's unpleasant,
especially when looking into the eyes of the man
you're killing. Oh and don't forget the torture,
and an incendiary shotgun that burns while it
eviscerates.[128]

Not only does it make killing a social activity, just like
playing ball hockey with your buddies, these companies
have made killing ironic, with heart-shaped red sight spots
as one of the customization options for your gun. Realism
has become a euphemism for how beautifully arterial blood

[127] Activision Publishing, Inc. "Press Releases," *Activision/Blizzard*,
http://investor.activision.com/releasedetail.cfm?ReleaseID=538246 (accessed:
January 28, 2011).
[128] "Call of Duty: Black Ops." *Playstation: Official Magazine (UK)*, Issue 51
(2010), p. 85.

gushes from chest wounds. Death has become a way to inject life into the game world. Murder is vitality.[129]

Should this be part of a normal, everyday life?

There's a game entitled *Dead Island*, and many game reviewers have described the trailer as chilling. It is possibly one of the most disturbing games I have ever seen. The game is being promoted as a first-person zombie-slasher/action RPG, so judging by the trailer and promotion this will be a conversation for our youth come late summer/early fall. *The Daily* (an iPad newspaper app) provided some interesting commentary on the trailer and the zombie genre.

> [There] is this continually replayed scene where you see someone who looks an awful lot like your girlfriend, or in this case your daughter, but it isn't her at all. It's about when we have to draw the lines between what's human and what's monster... If Dead Island can teach that society takes life for granted, then the use of the image is justified. If it turns out that it's merely a trashy horror game that used the image of a dead child to cause chatter and create hype, then the verdict will change.[130]

When is violence in video games going to change from being the norm to being the exception? It will be hard to change until extreme violence in video games stops creating

---

[129] Bissell, Tom. *Extra Lives: Why Video Games Matter* (New York, NY: Pantheon Books, 2010), p. 135.

[130] Thier, David. "The Living Dread," www.thedaily.com/page/2011/02/14/021811-apps-deadisland-controversy-1-2/ (accessed: February 22, 2011).

hype and anticipation, which drives video game sales. It won't be until we say enough is enough and that violence, whether on the screen or in the home, is unacceptable. The last time I checked, zombies were not an active part of my daily worldview, so why have they become a staple on the screens in our homes?

I cannot talk about violence in culture without talking once again about Grand Theft Auto. Do you remember the girl we talked about earlier from the game? That's right, the girl you can have sex with well after that you kill her and get your money back. This scene is written into the game. It is the game. Someone sat down and coded that result out. When we golf club a woman in the face in the game, someone during development golf-clubbed a dummy and recorded how it would look. The cheekbone breaks, blood comes out of her face (which was chosen from a colour pallet), and she crumbles to the ground. When we kick her on the ground, someone actually kicked something like a sack of potatoes and recorded what it looks like. It sounds foolish, but that girl becomes just as valuable as the sack of potatoes on the ground. When she is dead, you get paid. Welcome to Grand Theft Auto.

I really believe that you cannot tell me you oppose violence against women and play this game, or any other game like it. I stand by that and no one has ever given me a suitable argument against that statement. If you do not believe it, write me an email. My contact information is at the back of the book. Start your email with this line:

"Brett, I believe I can club a women in the face because..."

Have you ever been bullied?

Did you like it?

How did it make you feel?

Would you like to relive the experience in a video game?

Another game I would like to talk about is called Bully. As someone who speaks to numerous victims of bullying, I have to ask if this game is necessary. I deal with kids who are taking their own lives because someone told them their shoes are from Wal-Mart. So what is our answer to this growing dilemma? We bring out a game where we bully people for fun and entertainment. I don't know how that is fun. Bullying becomes justified to thousands of kids who play this game, because now it is fun. This becomes a normal part of their daily routine.

> To wake up each day knowing that you have to go to school, knowing there's no way of avoiding it, knowing that the moment you set out for school the bullies are there, waiting for you to arrive, waiting to call you names, to tease you, torment you, humiliate and mock you, embarrass you in front of friends, push you, punch you, slap you, pinch you, spit on you, kick you, and... you daren't think about the rest, or the possible consequences.[131]

I don't know how that is fun. Bullying becomes justified to thousands of kids who play this game, because now it is fun. This becomes a normal part of their daily routine.

---

[131] Marr, Neil and Tim Field. *Bullycide: Death at Playtime* (Didcot, UK: Success Unlimited, 2001), p. 250.

How can we help change the bullying and cyber bullying epidemic that is becoming the norm in our schools? That's easy. By educating ourselves and our youth on the basics of bullying.

- What is bullying?
- How should you respond to it?
- How can you avoid the situation?
- What is the next step? Who can help?

There are excellent online resources for cyber bullying awareness and bully prevention. They are geared towards both parents and youth.

- www.b-free.ca
- www.bullyingcanada.ca
- www.stopcyberbullying.org
- www.cyberbullying.us
- www.kidsafe.me
- www.iengage.ca

The culture of bullying in our schools, in our churches, and over the internet will only continue to grow if we don't begin to educate ourselves about what bullying looks like and how bullying affects kids. We need to be on the lookout for the symptoms of bullying. This problem will only improve when we begin to fully understand it. If we aren't educated about it, we could end up taking part in the hurt our kids are experiencing.

> If online bullying is being treated as the new kid
> on the block, that's probably not a bad thing. It's
> a cousin of all the old forms of meanness, but it's
> also causing trouble in new ways that we need to
> understand. Because cyberbullying is so easy, it
> may draw in kids who wouldn't shout insults in
> the cafeteria or spread a slut rumor while
> hanging out with friends after school. Press a
> button, and your jeering text or e-mail—or nude
> photo—can go out to the whole school. You can
> do this while feeling distant from the cruelty. You
> can do it without thinking. You can do it without
> a clique of mean girls (or guys) to egg you on. All
> of this hits teenagers in a developmental weak
> spot, playing on their young brains' tendency to
> act on impulse.[132]

It's up to us as parents and youth workers to help our kids navigate the dangers they face everyday in their lives, and that includes educating ourselves in preventing these dangers.

Where are we going as individuals when the games keep getting darker and more violent? Do you have a limit with violence and video games? What are your favourite games? What do they say about you?

I am not saying that all games are wrong. I grew up with the video game with the red–and–blue guns where you had to shoot the robbers—and not the innocent people— during a bank robbery. I suppose that was killing, in a sense.

---

[132] Bazelon, Emily. "Bull-E: Have You Been Cyberbullied," *Slate*, www.slate.com/id/2242666 (accessed: February 22, 2011).

Then there are games where you blow each other's heads off and blood covers the screen. Somewhere between the innocence of cops and robbers and the brutality of today's video games there needs to be a balance.

Movies have always been violent. The whole argument that they are getting more violent is not exactly true. Some of the original violent movies are the most violent, like *Reservoir Dogs, Clockwork Orange*, and *Seven. Psycho*, by Alfred Hitchcock, is another, but it didn't really portray violence. You never see the knife go into Janet Leigh's character. You never see it, it was perceived. *The Shining*, which I now call a comedy by today's standards, was quite violent when it was made in 1980.

MOVIE	RELEASE DATE	RATING
Alien	May 25, 1979	Rated R for sci-fi violence/gore and language.
A Clockwork Orange	February 2, 1972	Rated R for strong sexual content and violence throughout including rape, graphic nudity, and drug use. All involving teenagers.
Friday the 13th	May 9, 1980	Rated R for graphic bloody violence, sexuality, and some drug use.
Halloween	October 25, 1978	Rated R for strong violence and terror, language, some sexuality/nudity, and drug use.

MOVIE	RELEASE DATE	RATING
Nightmare on Elm Street	November 16, 1984	Rated R for horror violence, language, and some disturbing images.
Psycho	August 25, 1960	Rated R for violence.
Reservoir Dogs	October 23, 1992	Rated R for strong violence and language.
Seven	September 22, 1995	Rated R for strong graphic violence, some nudity, and pervasive language.
The Texas Chainsaw Massacre	October 1, 1974	Rated R for intense sequences of terror and violent content.
Texas Chainsaw Massacre 2	August 22, 1986	Unrated.
The Shining	May 23, 1980	Rated R.

*All movie info from www.imdb.com.

As we move forward, you have movies like *American History X, Gladiator, Fight Club,* and the highest grossing R-rated movie so far—*The Passion of the Christ.* That's right. Mel Gibson's portrayal of Jesus' sacrifice is the highest grossing restricted film of all time. Every time we see a new violent movie, we see something new and different. Those "ah moments" take away the disturbed feeling the next time you see it. For myself, one of those moments was when the guy gets shot in the car in *Pulp Fiction.* The movie *Wanted,* staring Angelina Jolie, was called a ballet of brutality as it was violence played out in poetic beauty that changed the way action sequences will be shot forever. *The Departed* also provided some of those as well. The point, though, is from that moment on we are okay with what happened in the film. The next time we see it on film, we will not think twice; it will just be another scene in some movie we watched at some point in our lives.

MOVIE	RELEASE DATE	RATING
American History X	October 30, 1998	Rated R for graphic and brutal violence including rape, pervasive language, strong sexuality, and nudity.
American Psycho	April 14, 2000	Rated R for strong violence, sexuality, drug use, and language.
Fight Club	October 15, 1999	Rated R for disturbing and graphic depictions of violent anti-social behaviour, sexuality, and language.
Gladiator	May 5, 2000	Rated R for intense, graphic combat.
Hannibal	February 9, 2001	Rated R for strong gruesome violence, some nudity, and language.
Kill Bill, Volume 1	October 10, 2003	Rated R for strong bloody violence, language, and some sexual content.
Kill Bill, Volume 2	April 16, 2004	Rated R for violence, language, and brief drug use.
Natural Born Killers	August 26, 1994	Rated R for extreme violence and graphic carnage, shocking images, strong language, and sexuality

MOVIE	RELEASE DATE	RATING
The Passion of the Christ	February 25, 2004	Rated R for sequences of graphic violence.
Pulp Fiction	October 14, 1994	Rated R for strong and graphic violence, drug use, pervasive strong language, and some sexuality.
Red Dragon	October 4, 2002	Rated R for violence, grisly images, language, some nudity, and sexuality.
Saving Private Ryan	July 24, 1998	Rated R for intense prolonged realistically graphic sequences of war violence and for language.
The Departed	October 6, 2006	Rated R for strong and brutal violence, pervasive language, strong sexual content, and drug material.
The Silence of the Lambs	February 14, 1991	Rated R for strong bloody violence, disturbing images, language, and some sexual content.

Everything changed with *Hostel.* After the torturous scenes displayed in *Hostel,* producers began to question whether or not those types of scenes would produce a new genre of film. With the introduction of intense torture in *Hostel*, the door was opened for producers and directors to expose their audiences to new forms of grotesque violence. This birthed a whole new genre of film called "torture porn." You can add all the *Saw* films, *The Hills Have Eyes*,

The Mist, and *Turistas* to this category. Reactions to *Hostel* were just as intense as the scenes in the movie.

> At the very first screening of "Hostel" at the 2005 Toronto Film Festival, two separate ambulances were called from people having such extreme reactions to the film. One man left the theater during Josh's torture, fainted, and tumbled down the escalator, and during Paxton's torture a woman had festival volunteers call an ambulance, claiming the film was giving her a heart attack. Both patrons were okay, and local media thought it was a publicity stunt by director Eli Roth. Ironically, Roth knew nothing of the incident, as he was in the theater watching the film, and only found out after when he was told by the festival staff of the chaos that transpired.[133]

We have to start questioning ourselves on the movies we watch when they start to invoke such strong reactions when we see them. Yes, it was only two people out of a whole theatre, but does that not make you wonder if we really need to expose ourselves to such graphic and unnatural scenarios?

---

[133] Internet Movie Database, "Trivia for Hostel," http://www.imdb.com/title/tt0450278/trivia?tr0781144 (accessed August 8, 2010).

brett ullman

MOVIE	RELEASE DATE	RATING
Hostel	January 6, 2006	Rated R for brutal scenes of torture and violence, strong sexual content, language, and drug use.
Planet Terror	June 21, 2007	Rated R for strong and graphic bloody violence throughout, sexual content, nudity, drug material, and pervasive language.
Halloween Unrated	August 31, 2007	Rated R for strong and brutal bloody violence and terror throughout, sexual content, graphic nudity, and language.
300	March 9, 2007	Rated R for graphic battle sequences throughout, some sexuality, and nudity.
Hostel, Part 2	June 8, 2007	Rated R for sadistic scenes of torture and bloody violence, terror, nudity, sexual content, language, and some drug content.
Pan's Labyrinth	January 19, 2007	Rated R for graphic violence and some language.
The Devil's Rejects	July 22, 2005	Rated R for sadistic violence, strong sexual content, language, and drug use.
Pineapple Express	August 8, 2008	Rated R for pervasive language, drug use, sexual references, and violence.

MOVIE	RELEASE DATE	RATING
Resident Evil: Extinction	September 21, 2007	Rated R for strong horror violence throughout and some nudity.
Rambo	January 25, 2008	Rated R for strong and graphic bloody violence, sexual assaults, grisly images, and language.
Saw 1–5	October 29, 2004– October 28, 2008	Rated R for strong and grisly violence and language. (*Saw 1* was edited for re-rating; it was originally NC-17).
Shoot 'Em Up	September 7, 2007	Rated R for pervasive and strong bloody violence, sexuality, and some language.
The Hills Have Eyes	March 10, 2006	Rated R for strong and gruesome violence and terror throughout, and language.
The Hills Have Eyes 2	March 23, 2007	Rated R for prolonged sequences of strong and gruesome horror violence and gore, rape, and language.
The Mist	November 21, 2007	Rated R for violence, terror and gore, and language.
Turistas	December 1, 2006	Rated R for strong and graphic violence and disturbing content, sexuality, nudity, drug use, and language.
Untraceable	January 25, 2008	Rated R for grisly violence and torture, and some language.

MOVIE	RELEASE DATE	RATING
Wanted	June 27, 2008	Rated R for strong bloody violence throughout, pervasive language, and some sexuality.
Kick Ass	April 16, 2010	Rated R for strong and brutal violence throughout, pervasive language, sexual content, nudity, and drug use—some involving children.

When I have to explain something, I have to ask if I am missing the mark. The point to all this is whether or not we are questioning what we are watching. Are we aware of what these movies portray as being acceptable? Are we aware that the movies we watch change how we view the world?

Let me be brutally honest about violence for a moment. You did not hear me say that if you play GTA (Grand Theft Auto), you will shoot up your school. I cannot tell you how many times people have come to my talks and have heard things I did not say. I do not want that to happen with this book. There are tens of millions of copies of GTA sold around the world and you cannot give me five hundred school shootings in the same time period.

We as Christians need to respond to the world with a smart yet rash commentary. Instead, too often the commentaries we give are reactionary and instantaneous. We see GTA or *Saw* as violent, and then make the conclusion that all violence stems from the increase in violent media. Countless times, a newspaper reports a school shooting and then trot out a Christian who says it is because of Grand Theft Auto. I didn't say that if you watch *Saw* or *Dexter*, you are going to go out and beat someone up. I do not think that is true.

I have been researching this for two years and do not think the root issue in violence is the media itself; the root is found in men. Men are responsible for 98.2% percent of the rapes in the world. Almost all domestic abusers are men. Men lead most violent statistics in the world. Men are the leaders responsible for almost every negative thing that happens on the planet. If we are going to have a real talk about violence, we need to turn away from media and start looking at the men of the world. Most men believe that domination and power over women, and everybody else, is normal. Look at GTA: the lead character is a male. Look at Manhunt, Bully, Gears of War, Soldier of Fortune, or almost any other violent video game or movie out there— the aggressor is usually a male. Do women commit violent acts? Of course, but I believe the root is male.

Kanye West's video for *Monster* was leaked to the internet near the end of 2010, and it contains some of the most disturbing content regarding women and abuse. The video was never officially released, but the content featured Kanye, Jay-Z, and Nicki Minaj performing in front of models hanging from the ceiling, severed body parts, and dead models lying in chairs. The Coalition Against Trafficking Women in Australia was one of the first groups to sponsor a petition against the video, claiming:

> The music industry's portrayals of women's pain,
> suffering, abuse, objectification, and victimization
> as valid forms of entertainment are not
> acceptable... The clip is not only interested in
> fetishizing female bodies, it revels in fetishizing
> female pain, female passivity, female suffering
> and female silence. The ultimate female is the
> quiet, passive female, a mannequin who accepts
> violence, abuse and suffering while remaining
> hot and sexy.[134]

The same article references Tracy Clark-Flory from *Salon*, whose words sum up the problem found within the video and our perception of culture today: "West offers a fascinating Rorschach test of our current sexual culture."[135] We need to present our youth with a correct worldview that speaks out against misogynistic viewpoints.

Jackson Katz is one of America's leading anti-sexist male activists, and on his website he points out ten ways that males can help stop gender violence. His first step reinforces the male role in gender violence. "Approach gender violence as a MEN'S issue involving men of all ages and socioeconomic, racial and ethnic backgrounds. View men not only as perpetrators or possible offenders, but as empowered bystanders who can confront abusive peers."[136] I

[134] Elser, Daniela. "Is Kanye West's *Monster* the Sickest Video Clip Ever?" http://www.news.com.au/entertainment/music/is-kanye-wests gruesome-monster-video-torture-porn-or-art/story-e6frfn09-1225993402801#ixzz1DxTMfNKc (accessed: February 10, 2011).
[135] Ibid.
[136] Katz, Jackson. "Ten Things Men Can Do to Prevent Gender Violence ," *Jackson Katz*, 1999, http://www.jacksonkatz.com/wmcd.html (accessed August 10, 2010).

hope we can all realize that male bashing is not my intent, nor is it the solution to this issue. It goes back to what we discussed earlier about abuse being selective and controllable.

If we just stopped here, if I just said "Good luck, glad you read this book," I would be wasting your time. The next question becomes, "Now what?"

FAITH

faith

We push our youth to higher education, but how often do we push our students to take care of their spiritual lives? We will spend and borrow tens of thousands of dollars to help make money for the future and invest so little to grow as believers. The pressure to seek wealth and worldly success before spiritual growth is seen everywhere, even from Christian parents and churches.[137]

his quote should cause us to ask some tough questions as we dive into the topic of faith. It should cause us to ask about what's important in the lives of our children. It should make us question our roles in maintaining and encouraging the spiritual lives of our kids.

---

[137] Sawler, David. *Goodbye Generation* (Surrey, BC: Ponder Publishing, 2009), p. 138.

We need to value the education of our kids outside the church, but why do we often place their education over our own spiritual growth? I'm not saying that their education and spiritual growth isn't important, but as parents we need to set examples of what a healthy spiritual life looks like. In order to be an example, we need to ensure that our spiritual growth is attended to. As we look beyond the culture that has influenced our lives, we should ask ourselves, "Now what? Where do we go from here?"

Let's start with this question: what is God saying to you where you are now?

I challenge everyone to read a book called *It: How Churches and Leaders Can Get It and Keep It*, by Craig Groeschel. In it, he says this about having "it":

> *It* doesn't stick any better to a young, hip, shaved-headed pastor with rimmed glasses, a goatee, and tattoos than it does to an older, stately gentlemen in a robe. Nor is *it* spotlights and lasers, video production, satellite dishes, fog machines, shiny gauze backdrops, four-color glossy brochures, sexy billboards, loud "contemporary" music, free donuts, coffee shops, hip bookstores, break dancing or acrobatics, sermon series named after television shows, a retro-modern matching chair and table onstage, or blue jeans and Heelys. *It* is *not* being on television, being on the internet, or being on book and magazine covers.[138]

---

[138] Groeschel, Craig. *It: How Churches and Leaders Can Get It and Keep It* (Grand Rapids, MI: Zondervan, 2008), p. 30.

The book is a great reminder that we're not called to form cookie-cutter churches. God calls you, God gives you a vision, God gives you a great work to do. We need to start looking at what God is calling you to do in your church, in your place. We need to start placing an importance on vision within our youth ministries.

> Seek God. Hear from God. Receive his vision. Let it overwhelm you. Consume you. Burden you. Tell the vision. Cast the vision. Communicate the vision. And watch it spread.[139]

Proverbs 29:18 says, *"If people can't see what God is doing, they stumble all over themselves; But when they attend to what he reveals, they are most blessed."* Vision should reflect the strengths of your young people or church body so that they can become confident in their faith and understanding of God's work in their lives. Vision gives the church meaning, identity, and most importantly it sends us out to do God's work in our communities, homes, and workplaces—not to mention in the church itself.

When we start casting vision, we stop being the Vanilla Church. After all, the world has a thousand flavors and we're only offering one. There is no Pentecostal, Baptist, CRC, or Mennonite churches anymore, because everyone is looking for *it* in the same ways and through the same cookie-cutter visions of church.

Every Sunday across North America, you hear the same songs (such as from Hillsong and Chris Tomlin). We preach

---

[139] Ibid., p. 48.

the same sermon series with little tweaks here and there. We all read the same books, by the same authors, and we wonder why we all have the same ideas. We have become the Vanilla Church: plain, bland, and uniform in all we do every week.

Gordon Mackenzie tells a story that speaks to this type of blind following. The story took place on his farm in 1904. One Sunday, after his two boys faked being sick to get out of church, one of the boys asked the other if he knew how to mesmerize a chicken. He then took a chicken out to the front porch and drew a short chalk outline on the ground in front of the chicken. The chicken was then placed on the line and its head held down. As he slowly removed his hand from in front of the chicken, the chicken stood motionless, staring beak-down at the chalk line.

The boys, being boys, continued doing this until the whole henhouse was empty. When all was said and done, there were seventy chickens with their beaks pointed down at the chalk, perfectly straddling the line. It wasn't until the parents came home and kicked the chickens into consciousness that they left that line.[140]

Just like those chickens, we've been mesmerized into an idea of church from which we cannot remove our sights— even if that means our progression of faith is stopped short and our churches fall.

> How easy is it for church to be pushed down to
> the chalk line and made to embrace the

---

[140] Frost, Michael. *Exiles: Living Missionally in a Post-Christian Culture* (Peabody, MA: Hendrickson Publishers, 2006), p. 52.

> philosophies, procedures, and politics of that empire? To continue with Macenzie's imagery, the wonderful thing that the dangerous stories of Jesus does is to place-kick us off the porch, to snap us back to consciousness and remind us of reality.[141]

We need to change everything. Now, when I say that, people just look at me and say, "Oh, you're one of those emerging church people." I don't even think that's an acceptable assumption to make. I say that things need to change because I want to escape the Vanilla Church. I just think that the status quo is no longer acceptable.

Seth Godin, in his book *Poke the Box,* says it well: "The job isn't to catch up to the status quo; the job is to invent the status quo."[142] If the church is going to grow and thrive today, it needs to strive to reinvent the whole idea of status quo.

We are all emerging; the church is and has always been emerging, because emerging simply refers to change. The church has been changing for two thousand years.

I have always believed that the church can emerge and change over the course of time. The church has continued to emerge over the last two thousand years, and it looks very different than it did in the second, fifth, fifteenth, or even twentieth century. We are not the same church! In that sense, I would consider myself emerging.

Fifty years ago, your church was probably debating whether or not drums were okay. Most churches today find

[141] Ibid., p. 53.
[142] Godin, Seth. *Poke the Box* (Irvington, NY: The Domino Project, 2011).

drums to be okay, but the fact is that it was a hot, emerging topic fifty years ago. I was once in a church that called an emergency deacons meeting because someone had moved the drums from one side of the stage to another. When will we have the opportunity to engage in *real* ministry if we spend our time in deacon meetings discussing the placement of the drum kit?

The other problem with labeling churches and leaders as "emergent" or "emerging" is that they are broad titles that could mean a variety of things to a variety of different people. Mark Driscoll, in an article entitled "A Pastoral Perspective of the Emergent Church," breaks down this broad understanding into three different subtitles. The first group he calls *relevants*:

> *Relevants* are theologically conservative evangelicals who are not as interested in reshaping theology as much as updating such things as worship styles, preaching styles, and church leadership structures.[143]

Becoming relevant to new generations of church attendees is one of their biggest focuses, and that gives them a big postmodern following. They can also be viewed as implementing and searching for new trends without seeing a distinct conversion process happening within their church.

The second group that Driscoll points out is the *reconstructionists*.

---

[143] Driscoll, Mark. "A Pastoral Perspective on the Emerging Church," *Scribd*, www.scribd.com/doc/190605/A-Pastoral-Perspective-on-the-Emergent-Church (accessed: April 4, 2011).

> They bolster their critique by noting that our
> nation is becoming less Christian and that those
> who profess faith are not living lives markedly
> different than non-Christians; thereby, proving
> that current church forms have failed to create
> life transformation.[144]

One of the driving forces of *reconstructionists* is less formal, smaller group settings, which have a focus on incarnational churches. They tend to meet in smaller *communitas*, as Alan Hirsch refers to in *The Forgotten Ways*.

> The related ideas of liminality and communitas
> describe the dynamics of the Christian
> community inspired to overcome their instincts
> to "huddle and cuddle," and to instead form
> themselves around a common mission that calls
> them onto a dangerous journey to unknown
> places, a mission that calls the church to shake off
> its collective securities and to plunge into the
> world of action.[145]

This group does not use a megachurch model and would rather look to a smaller church model.

The third and last group are the *revisionists*.

> Revisionists are theologically liberal and question
> key evangelical doctrines, critiquing their

---

[144] Ibid.

[145] Hirsch, Alan. *The Forgotten Ways: Reactiviating the Missional Church* (Grand Rapids, MI: Brazos Press, 2006), p. 277.

appropriateness for the emerging postmodern world.[146]

The *revisionists* address such topics as the atonement, the reality of hell, and the nature of the Gospel, among other topics.

It's about time we started to look at what isn't working in church and change it. We don't change everything. We don't change the sovereignty of Christ, we don't change the virgin birth, and we don't go changing the Trinity. The things that we change are the areas that aren't working.

One area that needs changing is the way our teens view God and how he works in their lives.

> Moralistic Therapeutic Deism makes no pretense at changing lives; it is a low commitment, compartmentalized set of attitudes aimed at "meeting my needs" and "making me happy" rather than bending my life into a pattern of love and obedience to God.[147]

If the church we've given them isn't changing lives, then isn't it about time we change the vision and look of what has brought us to this point?

> Teenagers tend to view God as either a butler or a therapist, someone who meets their needs

---

[146] Driscoll, Mark. "A Pastoral Perspective on the Emerging Church," *Scribd*, www.scribd.com/doc/190605/A-Pastoral-Perspective-on-the-Emergent-Church (accessed: April 4, 2011).
[147] Dean, Kendra Creasy. *Almost Christian: What The Faith Of Our Teenagers Is Telling The American Church* (New York, NY: Oxford University Press, 2010), pp. 29–30.

> when summoned... or who listens
> nonjudgmentally and helps youth feel good
> about themselves.[148]

We have been arguing this point for almost twenty years now. We have been arguing over the reasons why churches all over North America are closing their doors, losing members, and why people are leaving their faith for other belief structures. The argument has led us nowhere, because it has all been words without action, because we are scared to emerge and change as a church.

Whether the argument is about when young adults leave the church or how we bring them back, the solution is the same: change or die.

Kendra Creasy Dean points out three quick solutions for how to keep the church body, especially the young adult demographic, engaged and living out their faith. They are translation, testimony, and detachment.[149]

Translation, simply put, is mentorship—adults who mentor youth on the language and practices of the church in order for them to participate within a community of believers.

Testimony is about teaching youth to articulate their faith with clear understanding, so that they can confess and live out their biblical worldview in their smaller communities—such as school and after-school programs.

Detachment is about teaching and participating in the spiritual disciplines that take the focus off of us and place it back on Christ.

---

[148] Ibid., p. 17.
[149] Ibid., p. 23.

Until we start consciously placing younger Christians within our vision of church, we are working from the definition of insanity—doing the same things for years, expecting something to click. When it doesn't, we go back and start at the same point with the same question: where are all our young people and can we survive without them?

What do we do with this information?

How do we move forward?

These questions need to be reflective responses to the cultural influences that surround us every day. If movies, music, and video games are how we see the world working around us, how do we change that? When God's original calling on our lives has been lost in lyrics, ballads, and scripts, how do we get back to that calling? The question—"Now what?"—then becomes a personal journey back to our creator. The only way we can get back to our creator is by acting out our beliefs.

Kary Oberbrunner, in *Called: Becoming Who You Were Born to Be*, explains how beliefs can be integrated into our lives. In Hebrew philosophy, a belief is not a belief until it is acted on. All beliefs affect community because the actions they spawn affect every area of life.[150] This is a challenge for many of us as we go about putting our beliefs into actions. When we move away from this challenge, or fail to engage, we fall into the very dangerous trap of misleading others and ourselves into who Jesus is and what he has called us to do.

---

[150] Oberbrunner, Kary. *Called: Becoming Who You Were Born to Be* (Winona Lake, IN: BMH Books, 2007), p. 54.

"I think we have bought into a new Jesus who allows us to live our lives any way we desire."[151]

Paul warns us about this trap in his letter to the Colossians: *"See to it that no one takes you captive through hollow and deceptive philosophy, which depends on human tradition and the basic principles of this world rather than on Christ"* (Colossians 2:8, NIV).

So, what now?

See the Plan

The first step is to let God's original calling and plan be revealed to us. How do we allow God's story to be revealed to us? Simply put, this is the Bible. It is God's word given to us as an instruction manual, the way to life, life in him. The Bible is meant to be our story—our story given to us by a loving God who is constantly at work in the world. "The Bible tells a story. A story that isn't over. A story that is still being told. A story that we have a part to play in."[152] We have been given an opportunity to be a part of God's story, but we need to understand why.

John Taylor, in *A Story-Shaped Faith*, explains how we are to best understand our roles.

> Do you want to understand yourself? Do you want to know the meaning of life, or what you are meant to do? Let me tell you a story: "In the beginning God..." That is the opening line of the

[151] Ibid., p. 9.
[152] Bell, Rob *Velvet Elvis: Repainting the Christian Faith* (Grand Rapids, MI: Zondervan, 2005), p. 66.

story of God's relationship with his creation. In
the story, we have both rights and
responsibilities. One of those responsibilities is
to remember what God has done and tell it to
the next generation.[153]

What does God's word say about this idea of storytelling?

God's Message to Joel son of Pethuel:
Attention, elder statesmen! Listen closely,
everyone, whoever and wherever you are!
Have you ever heard of anything like this?
Has anything like this ever happened before—
     ever?
Make sure you tell your children,
and your children tell their children,
and their children their children.
Don't let this message die out. (Joel 1:1–3)

Write this down for the next generation so
people not yet born will praise God. (Psalms
102:18)

And then he told the People of Israel, "In the
days to come, when your children ask their
fathers, 'What are these stones doing here?' tell
your children this: 'Israel crossed over this Jordan
on dry ground.' Yes, God, your God, dried up
the Jordan's waters for you until you had crossed,
just as God, your God, did at the Red Sea, which

---

[153] Taylor, Daniel. "A Story-Shaped Faith," in *The Power of Words and The
Wonder of God*, ed. John Piper: Justin Taylor, 105-121 (Wheaton, IL: Crossway
Books, 2009), p. 113.

had dried up before us until we had crossed."
(Joshua 4:21–23)

Place these words on your hearts. Get them
deep inside you. Tie them on your hands and
foreheads as a reminder. Teach them to your
children. Talk about them wherever you are,
sitting at home or walking in the street; talk
about them from the time you get up in the
morning until you fall into bed at night.
(Deuteronomy 11:18–20)

And do this so that their children, who don't yet
know all this, will also listen and learn to live in
holy awe before God, your God, for as long as
you live on the land that you are crossing over
the Jordan to possess. (Deuteronomy 31:13)

Take to heart all these words to which I give
witness today and urgently command your
children to put them into practice, every single
word of this Revelation. (Deuteronomy 32:46)

This way, your children won't be able to say to
our children in the future, "You have no part in
God." We said to ourselves, "If anyone speaks
disparagingly to us or to our children in the
future, we'll say: Look at this model of God's
Altar which our ancestors made. It's not for
Whole-Burnt-Offerings, not for sacrifices. It's a
witness connecting us with you." (Joshua 22:27–
28)

Then commanded our parents
to teach it to their children
So the next generation would know,
and all the generations to come—
Know the truth and tell the stories
so their children can trust in God,
Never forget the works of God
but keep his commands to the letter.
(Psalms 78:5–8)

"As for me," God says, "this is my covenant with
them: My Spirit that I've placed upon you and
the words that I've given you to speak, they're
not going to leave your mouths nor the mouths
of your children nor the mouths of your
grandchildren. You will keep repeating these
words and won't ever stop." God's orders. (Isaiah
59:21).

The people of Ephraim will be famous,
their lives brimming with joy.
Their children will get in on it, too—
oh, let them feel blessed by God!
I'll whistle and they'll all come running.
I've set them free—oh, how they'll flourish!
Even though I scattered them to the far corners
     of earth,
they'll remember me in the faraway places.
They'll keep the story alive in their children,
And they will come back. (Zechariah 10:7–10)

The promise is targeted to you and your
children, but also to all who are far away—

whomever, in fact, our Master God invites. (Acts
2:39)

Throughout Scripture, we are given a clear example
that God's ways will in fact be passed down through stories,
but how do we learn of his stories? It is simple—through
the discipline of study. Study has always seemed like such a
negative word when it comes to listening and learning the
words of God. This is because it holds so many negative
memories for us—the late nights studying for an exam, that
test we studied all night for and failed anyway, those
beautiful June afternoons lost to a world of textbooks.

However, when we study the word of God, the
connections with the world around us are nothing like the
dreadful days of June exams. Read aloud these words from
Rob Bell and listen to the transformation that can come
from reading and studying God's word. The world that
God's word invites us into is very much the world we are
trying to escape from. That is the beauty behind God's
story. As we try to escape from our lives, searching for
answers, he invites us into his story, which ironically is
happening all around us.

> We have to embrace the Bible as the wild,
> uncensored, passionate account it is of people
> experiencing the living God. Doubting the one
> true God. Wrestling with, arguing with, getting
> angry with, reconciling with, loving, worshiping,
> thanking, following the one who gives us
> everything. Real people, in real places, in real
> times, writing and telling stories about their

experiences and their growing understanding of
who God is and who they are.[154]

Are these not the questions we are seeking answers to?
Who am I?
Where am I?
What am I doing here?

Experience

When we study God's word on a personal level, we begin
to experience, to be able to apprehend the objects, people,
events, thoughts, and emotions that we read on the pages.
Our senses, thoughts, and experiences begin to take shape
before us and we get to personally participate in God's
story. This type of learning, or experiencing, is the best way
for us to transform our actions based on the beliefs we hold.
"The only kind of learning which significantly influences
behavior is self discovered, or self appropriated learning—
this is truth assimilated in experience."[155] God meets us on
the page in a personal way as we begin to understand our
own experiences and God's truths begin to show themselves
in our daily lives.

Tony Jones explains discipline and the benefits of
studying God's word. "Christians engage in these spiritual
practices not out of duty or obligation but because there is a
promise attached: God will personally meet us in the midst

[154] Bell, Rob. *Velvet Elvis: Repainting the Christian Faith* (Grand Rapids, MI:
Zondervan, 2005), p. 63.
[155] Miller, Mark. *Experiential Storytelling: (Re)discovering Narrative to
Communicate God's Message* (El Cajon, CA: Zondervan, 2003), p.17.

of these disciplines."[156] This is where our theology forms. We begin to understand the character and nature of our God as we study his words and personally and emotionally experience what he continues to do. The Bible teaches us who he is, what he is like, and what he intended us for. In the end, we begin to see that all stories point to our restoration through Jesus. As stories shape our imagination, we begin to see how big God truly is. Theology allows us to place the story within the meta-narrative.

There are a couple of big words in that last sentence that we should break down together.

Theology, in this sense, is not a deep and scientific word but a simple understanding of who God is through his nature and characteristics. We gain this understanding through what we talked about earlier—studying the word of God. Tony Jones explains how this type of theological outlook can benefit our understanding of God.

> And anytime human beings talk of God, they're necessarily also going to talk about their experience of God... In other words, it's how we talk about the points of intersection between God and us, the places where God's activity meets our activity.[157]

How else would we get to know someone better? We learn about God the same way we learn about our friends.

---

[156] Jones, Tony. *The Sacred Way: Spiritual Practices for Everyday Life* (Grand Rapids, MI: Zondervan, 2005), p. 18.

[157] Jones Tony, *The New Christians: Dispatches From the Emergent Frontier* (San Francisco, CA: Jossey-Bass, 2008), p. 105.

By talking with him, listening to his words, and understanding what he likes.

Meta-narrative is the next big word that we need to unpack in order to more fully understand how God works in the world. A meta-narrative is "a grand, overarching, all-encompassing story that gives meaning and order to life—past, present, and future."[158] When we begin to read about him with an intention to gain a better understanding of who he is, we begin to look more like him every day.

> I'm telling you to love your enemies. Let them bring out the best in you, not the worst. When someone gives you a hard time, respond with the energies of prayer, for then you are working out of your true selves, your God-created selves. (Matthew 5:44–45)

God asks us to make a transformation away from our true selves so that we can reflect him, and in doing so the scriptures start to become our story as well. When we read scriptures that talk about Jesus, or Jesus teaches us about himself, we need to also ask ourselves questions so that we can better understand him.

What does the story say about Jesus? What is, or who is, Jesus concerned with in the story? What does Jesus value in the story?

Who is Jesus?

Take the time to read the following passages and ask yourself the same questions.

---

[158] Novelli, Michael. *Shaped By The Story: Helping Students Encounter God in a New Way* (Grand Rapids , MI: Zondervan, 2008), p. 27.

> MATTHEW 25:40, MATTHEW 5:44–45,
> MATTHEW 9:13, MATTHEW 18:10–14, JOHN
> 8:12, LUKE 10:25–37, ACTS 20:35, MATTHEW
> 8:22, MATTHEW 25:41–45, LUKE 4:18–19,
> MATTHEW 22:37–40, MATTHEW 11:28–30,
> MATTHEW 25:31–40, MARK 10:17:22, JOHN
> 10:10–14, AND MATTHEW 16:25–28.

What did those passages say about who God is?

What does he value?

God values compassion. He values love, relationships, and life. Those are only a few of the things God values, but these are also the characteristics of God. When we read about his nature and characteristics, we can only strive to be like him.

Tom Davis, in his book *Red Letters: Living a Faith that Bleeds*, shows how understanding who God is will transform our lives by how others see us.

> Learning to live a faith that is so real, you bleed
> Jesus. Here's how you start: Look for Jesus every
> morning in the eyes of the people you meet.
> And then look for him in the mirror.[159]

Our search for Jesus needs to begin well before we wake up in the morning. It needs to start the moment we take the time to learn who he is and what he values most in us and in his creation. Paul, in Ephesians 4:1–3, tells us that God calls us to run, not walk, on the road God called us to, so

---

[159] Davis, Tom. *Red Letters: Living a Faith that Bleeds* (Colorado Springs, CO: David C. Cook, 2007), p. 28.

that we can be living examples of him. We can only do this, however, if we take the time to learn about him.

Identity Reversal

As we emerge with an understanding of who God is, we begin to go through an identity reversal. We begin to look up to God for an understanding of who we are instead of looking out into the world for acceptance and approval. We begin to make connections with the stories we read and experience emotions that link those stories of God to the stories of our life. We become folded into God's story by acting out our roles.

Our identity reversal can only come once we embrace the idea that the way we make decisions, and the source of our identity, has changed over the years. Instead of looking to our creator for guidance and our own outlooks of self, we have looked out into culture for identity. God's creation story tells us that we need to take part in a reverse engineering of our lives. We need to move towards and maintain a lifestyle that says we are created in his image, not Zac Efron's. The Bible should be our source of inspiration and the source of truth—not MTV or Much Music. Do we base our wardrobe decisions on what we can afford, what looks best on our bodies, and is modest? Or do we base our wardrobes on what we see in the music videos, magazines, and billboards that surround us every day?

> God created human beings; he created them
> godlike, reflecting God's nature. He created

them male and female. God blessed them:
"Prosper! Reproduce! Fill Earth! Take charge! Be
responsible for fish in the sea and birds in the air,
for every living thing that moves on the face of
Earth." (Genesis 1:27–28)

We are given a very distinct calling in Genesis to reflect
God's nature. We talked about this earlier and it is
extremely difficult to reflect this nature without changing
the source of our identity. Mark Sayers takes the idea of
reverse engineering our lives and gives a basis for change in
his book, *The Vertical Self*:

> The horizontal self looks to others for a sense of
> identity rather than to something larger than
> oneself, thus finding a sense of self in one's status
> within society. With God playing no real
> authoritative role in informing identity, people
> look to others as the ultimate judge. Whereas
> the vertical self looks to heaven for favor and
> approval, the horizontal self looks to the world
> for approval and acceptance. For people who
> hold a horizontal sense of self, the creation and
> cultivation of a public image are paramount.[160]

It takes everything we have talked about so far to get to
this point. Reading the Bible helps us to find the source of
our identity. Understanding who God is and what God
stands for allows us to see that his image is the one we
should strive to reflect every day.

---

[160] Sayers, Mark. *The Vertical Self* (Nashville, TN: Thomas Nelson, 2010), p. 17.

Reverse engineering our lives requires us to proclaim a few things that may be difficult for us to admit: He is big and we are not. He will be the ultimate judge, not Simon Cowell or anyone else. His ways are forever; the world's ways are temporary. We are okay with gratification that comes at a later date.

With the emergence of our new selves, we begin to live out our lives and stories within a new community. This new community is larger, more inviting, and more accepting because it is a community centered in God. This community evolves out of our Biblical worldview. In order to understand what a Biblical worldview looks like, we need to go all the way back to the line we drew earlier. Remember that?

The question we have to ask ourselves now is, what makes our line right? Is your line more right than my line? Maybe not, but one thing *does* make us right. It is being a Christian, a follower of the way; it is asking, what does the Bible say? Anything beyond that is merely justification—when we try to justify the way we act, what we say, and what we do every day without looking to see what the Bible says. If we have a biblical worldview, we will have biblical values. When we have biblical values, we will have biblical actions. We have to focus on each one of those steps, because without one the others fall apart.

Let me give you an example. I was speaking in an East Coast hockey arena, a few thousand people all around me, when a guy walked up, saying, "Brett, I got it."

My response was, "What?"

"I got it," he repeated, as if I had not heard him the first time. He puts his hand out to shake mine, but as he does he drops a bag of weed into it.

I am instantly uncomfortable. A few thousand people at this point just witnessed a drug deal and I am the one holding the bag of weed.

I looked at the guy and said, "You are an idiot. We talked about this." He has a son at home who smokes a lot of weed and we have talked about it over a long period of time. His solution to his son smoking pot is to go home, kick down his son's door, and take whatever pot his son has and give it to the speaker. Somehow that becomes the end solution to him. He has done nothing to help his son.

"Where's your son?" I ask.

"What do you mean?"

"Where's your son?"

"I don't know."

"He's out buying more drugs right now."

It's not about the little bag of weed but rather the question, "Why?" Why is your son getting drunk? Why is your son getting high? The root of the problem is not the action. It is the worldview. The root is found when we address why he believes it is okay to smoke pot. The action is affected by the worldview. All kidding aside, the son was probably out buying more weed at that point because the root issue was not addressed. That is the problem we have with worldviews today. We look at our actions without asking why we do the things we do.

Dallas Willard, the author of *The Spirit of the Disciples*, tells us how we can gain biblical worldviews. "We can become like Christ by practicing the types of activities he engaged in."[161] This, however, is a process. Mastering these activities does not happen overnight, but we can start practicing to be like Christ right away. Our worldviews will probably align in some ways, but differ in other areas. Worldviews act like glasses or contact lenses, because it is essentially the way in which we view the world and its contents. It is what allows us to make decisions about our line as we ask what is an acceptable, Godly outlook on the world around us.

When I fail to wear my God glasses, I'm left up to my own feelings and thoughts about faith,

[161] Willard, Dallas. *The Spirit of the Disciplines* (San Francisco, CA: Harper & Row, 1988), p. xi.

culture, and my role in both. With my glasses off,
I can justify and rationalize sinful habits, sins, and
philosophies that are a direct offense to God
and His Word. However, the moment I start to
filter life and culture through my own eyes is the
moment I find myself on a path I don't care to be
on.[162]

We would like to think we got it (our worldview) on
our own, that we assembled and examined all the evidence
and chose the worldview that was the most defensible or
"right," then proceeded to use that worldview as our
assumption for explaining things.

Sorry.

Most of us inherited our worldview. We got it from our
family, friends, the media, and our experiences. Even
Christians who claim to have gotten their worldview
directly from Scripture probably didn't. More likely, we
learned to approach Scripture with a worldview, thus even
what we found in Scripture was influenced by what we
expected to find. This "leads" our study of Scripture.

Paul warns us in Colossians that it is very easy for us to
get caught up in a worldview that is based upon culture.
*"See to it that no one takes you captive through hollow and
deceptive philosophy, which depends on human tradition and the
basic principles of this world rather than on Christ"* (Colossians
2:8).

[162] Oberbrunner, Kary. *The Journey Towards Relevence: Simple Steps for Transforming Your World* (Lake Mary, FL: Relevant Books, 2004), p. 125.

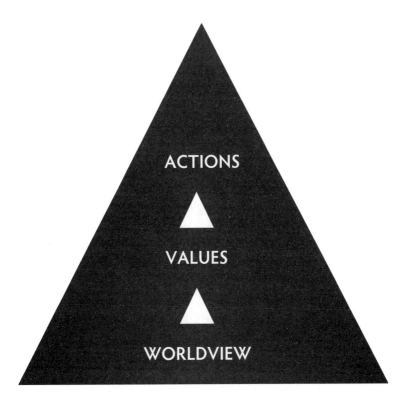

Our worldviews are integrated into our lives just like this pyramid. The young guy and his dad with the weed need to approach the problem in this order. Somewhere along the way, the son has gotten the message that smoking weed is either the cool thing to do, the solution to something, or he simply believes that it is the best choice for him. Where he got that message could be anywhere. It could be from friends, home, or through the messages found in some form of media. The son now thinks it is okay to smoke weed, so his values start to reflect that and then he acts upon those values and that worldview. The father, in order to fix this family issue, needs to address the root, which is where the son got the message that weed was a good option.

When we as adults have biblical worldviews, we start to eliminate things like adultery. Why? Because it goes against the biblical worldview that shapes our values and determines our actions. Adultery, when placed within our biblical worldviews, removes itself from the norm that society has placed on it through its depiction in the media.

Do you have a biblical worldview?

Let's use another example. It started with Napster. Napster gave way to sites like LimeWire, BitTorrent, and Kazaa. They're all the same; it doesn't matter the actual name, because they all allow you to pirate music for free.

As Canadians, we are amongst the biggest downloaders in the world. The Bible tells us one thing and our Supreme Court says something else. The Supreme Court says you can download, but the Bible says we shouldn't steal. It says, in Ephesians 4:28, *"Did you used to make ends meet by stealing? Well, no more!"*

If you don't own the rights to a song, you cannot download it. That's stealing. What's interesting today is how normal it is. I have walked into youth groups where people pass around burned music from BitTorrent, and it's not just the youth doing it; it's the youth pastor as well. We are giving a very mixed message at the point where we think that this is okay.

What about our thoughts? What would happen if we could plug a little remote into our brains that projected our thoughts onto a screen? What would happen every time an attractive person or colleague walked in front of us? Where did we look when we thought no one was looking?

Why are we here? Why do we run youth ministries? Why do we go to church? To build our biblical worldviews and to encourage the worldviews of the young people around us.

How do we prepare ourselves to be agents of transformation through our worldviews?

Community Living

The answer lies in community—not a community outside of culture, but a community that is engaged and participates within society and culture. A community based on the New Testament church, a church that is centered on the very essence of who God is.

Nate Larkin described this community in his book, *Samson and the Pirate Monks*. He bases community on three things: compassion, love, and helping hands.

> The church according to the New Testament is not a loose confederation of individuals. The church is a body—a living, breathing organism whose members are so intimately connected that they can only move together. On any given day, every member of that body needs help, and every member has some help to give.[163]

---

[163] Larkin, Nate. *Samson and the Pirate Monks: Calling Men to Authentic Brotherhood* (Nashville, TN: W Pub. Group, 2007), p. 73.

Our community, whether it is a church, friends, families, or simply the people we encounter every day in our local Starbucks, needs to become fluid, or even organic in nature. The values of Christ should flow out from us with ease and without hesitation. That is what an agent of transformation does best—allows their worldview to flow through them into the lives of those within their communities.

> The Christian movement must be the living breathing promise to live out the values of Christ—This is, to be a radical, troubling alternative to the power imbalance in the empire. In a world of greed and consumerism, the church ought to be a community of generosity and selflessness.[164]

The difficulty with reengineering our worldviews, our identity, and our need for true community lies in our feelings of insecurity. These insecurities may arise from making extreme changes in our lives. Moving beyond simply living in communities to being active participants and agents of transformation requires movement. Alan Hirsch, in *The Forgotten Ways*, concludes that, yes, movement and participation is difficult and full of insecurities—but this was, in fact, the way of the original Jesus revolution.

---

[164] Frost, Michael. *Exiles: Living Missionally in a Post-Christian Culture* (Peabody, MA: Hendrickson Publishers, 2006), p. 15.

That is not to say that every Christian literally left home and family to follow Jesus, but that the foundational spiritual transaction of laying down all in the name of Jesus was at the very base of all of their subsequent following. In this way they had made an abiding decision to enter into the liminality of leaving securities and comforts when they first became Christians and so didn't have to try and factor it in later. This meant that they remained a liquid people, consequently adapting and evolving, depending on context.[165]

What is the context of your community?

Is it family? Is it friends? Is it your workplace? Is it your local Starbucks?

Communities are wherever we go; they follow us because they are an extension of who we are and how we see the world. When we look to the Bible as our storyboard to discover who God is and then allow that information to change how we see the world and see what is right and true, God begins to flow out of us naturally to all those around us. That is the beauty of becoming an agent of transformation and the beauty of true community.

At this stage, story begins to penetrate our decisions and choices based upon our new worldview. This allows us to envision and live out our roles within creation. We join in as co-creators as we pray, socialize, serve, and are hospitable to those around us on a daily basis. We naturally begin to live like little Christs in our communities—and others take notice. They notice lives with meaning, happiness, and

---

[165] Hirsch, Alan. *The Forgotten Ways: Reactiviating the Missional Church* (Grand Rapids, MI: Brazos Press, 2006), p. 241.

purpose—lives that are in communion with our creator and restorer. We become followers of Jesus!

What is a follower of Jesus?

> Followers of Jesus are people who are committed to partnering with God to make this world, the world that we all live in, the kind of place that God originally intended it to be. In Jesus' precise words, we're learning to love each other as we love ourselves.[166]

What message did Paul bring to these new followers of Jesus and their communities? Paul engaged them where they were—personally, emotionally, spiritually, and culturally. He went into their towns, synagogues, home churches, and places of communion and community involvement. Paul entered their coffee shops, homes, arenas, and church buildings as a means of establishing relationships and creating and fostering healthy worldviews with new followers of Christ. Even today, the best way to understand the communities we live in is to go where the people are. That way, you can see what values determine their actions.

Paul's opening addresses to each community in his letters allows us to see how community shapes and moulds us, but it is our communal worldviews that keep us connected with each other and with God's larger plan of restoration.

> Every time I think of you—and I think of you often!—I thank God for your lives of free and

---

[166] Bell, Rob. *Discussion Guide 001* (Grand Rapids, MI: Zondervan, 2009), p. 63.

open access to God, given by Jesus. There's no
end to what has happened in you—it's beyond
speech, beyond knowledge. The evidence of
Christ has been clearly verified in your lives.

Just think—you don't need a thing, you've
got it all! All God's gifts are right in front of you
as you wait expectantly for our Master Jesus to
arrive on the scene for the Finale. And not only
that, but God himself is right alongside to keep
you steady and on track until things are all
wrapped up by Jesus. God, who got you started
in this spiritual adventure, shares with us the life
of his Son and our Master Jesus. He will never
give up on you. Never forget that. (1 Corinthians
1:4–9)

We're not in charge of how you live out the faith,
looking over your shoulders, suspiciously critical.
We're partners, working alongside you, joyfully
expectant. I know that you stand by your own
faith, not by ours. (2 Corinthians 1:24)

I can't believe your fickleness—how easily you
have turned traitor to him who called you by the
grace of Christ by embracing a variant message!
It is not a minor variation, you know; it is
completely other, an alien message, a no-
message, a lie about God. Those who are
provoking this agitation among you are turning
the Message of Christ on its head. Let me be
blunt: If one of us—even if an angel from
heaven!—were to preach something other than
what we preached originally, let him be cursed. I
said it once; I'll say it again: If anyone, regardless
of reputation or credentials, preaches something

other than what you received originally, let him be cursed. (Galatians 1:6–10)

It's in Christ that you, once you heard the truth and believed it (this Message of your salvation), found yourselves home free—signed, sealed, and delivered by the Holy Spirit. This signet from God is the first installment on what's coming, a reminder that we'll get everything God has planned for us, a praising and glorious life. That's why, when I heard of the solid trust you have in the Master Jesus and your outpouring of love to all the Christians, I couldn't stop thanking God for you—every time I prayed, I'd think of you and give thanks... your eyes focused and clear, so that you can see exactly what it is he is calling you to do, grasp the immensity of this glorious way of life he has for Christians, oh, the utter extravagance of his work in us who trust him—endless energy, boundless strength! ... He is in charge of it all, has the final word on everything. At the center of all this, Christ rules the church. The church, you see, is not peripheral to the world; the world is peripheral to the church. The church is Christ's body, in which he speaks and acts, by which he fills everything with his presence. (Ephesians 1:13–16, 18–19, 22–23)

I am so pleased that you have continued on in this with us, believing and proclaiming God's Message, from the day you heard it right up to the present. There has never been the slightest doubt in my mind that the God who started this great work in you would keep at it and bring it to

a flourishing finish on the very day Christ Jesus
appears... Learn to love appropriately. You need
to use your head and test your feelings so that
your love is sincere and intelligent, not
sentimental gush. Live a lover's life, circumspect
and exemplary, a life Jesus will be proud of:
bountiful in fruits from the soul, making Jesus
Christ attractive to all, getting everyone involved
in the glory and praise of God... Meanwhile, live
in such a way that you are a credit to the
Message of Christ. Let nothing in your conduct
hang on whether I come or not. Your conduct
must be the same whether I show up to see
things for myself or hear of it from a distance.
Stand united, singular in vision, contending for
people's trust in the Message, the good news,
not flinching or dodging in the slightest before
the opposition. Your courage and unity will show
them what they're up against: defeat for them,
victory for you—and both because of God.
There's far more to this life than trusting in
Christ. There's also suffering for him. And the
suffering is as much a gift as the trusting. You're
involved in the same kind of struggle you saw me
go through, on which you are now getting an
updated report in this letter. (Philippians 1:5–7,
9–12, 27–30)

You yourselves are a case study of what he does.
At one time you all had your backs turned to
God, thinking rebellious thoughts of him, giving
him trouble every chance you got. But now, by
giving himself completely at the Cross, actually
dying for you, Christ brought you over to God's
side and put your lives together, whole and holy

in his presence. You don't walk away from a gift
like that! You stay grounded and steady in that
bond of trust, constantly tuned in to the
Message, careful not to be distracted or
diverted. There is no other Message—just this
one. Every creature under heaven gets this same
Message. I, Paul, am a messenger of this
Message... The mystery in a nutshell is just this:
Christ is in you, therefore you can look forward
to sharing in God's glory. It's that simple. That is
the substance of our Message. We preach Christ,
warning people not to add to the Message. We
teach in a spirit of profound common sense so
that we can bring each person to maturity. To be
mature is to be basic. Christ! No more, no less.
That's what I'm working so hard at day after day,
year after year, doing my best with the energy
God so generously gives me. (Colossians 1:22–
24, 27–29)

You paid careful attention to the way we lived
among you, and determined to live that way
yourselves. In imitating us, you imitated the
Master. Although great trouble accompanied the
Word, you were able to take great joy from the
Holy Spirit!—taking the trouble with the joy, the
joy with the trouble... The news of your faith in
God is out. We don't even have to say anything
anymore—you're the message! People come up
and tell us how you received us with open arms,
how you deserted the dead idols of your old life
so you could embrace and serve God, the true
God. They marvel at how expectantly you await
the arrival of his Son, whom he raised from the

dead—Jesus, who rescued us from certain doom. (1 Thessalonians 1:5–7, 8–10)

If your life honors the name of Jesus, he will honor you. Grace is behind and through all of this, our God giving himself freely, the Master, Jesus Christ, giving himself freely. (2 Thessalonians 1:12)

The whole point of what we're urging is simply love—love uncontaminated by self-interest and counterfeit faith, a life open to God. Those who fail to keep to this point soon wander off into cul-de-sacs of gossip. They set themselves up as experts on religious issues, but haven't the remotest idea of what they're holding forth with such imposing eloquence. (1 Timothy 1:5–7)

So don't be embarrassed to speak up for our Master or for me, his prisoner. Take your share of suffering for the Message along with the rest of us. We can only keep on going, after all, by the power of God, who first saved us and then called us to this holy work. We had nothing to do with it. It was all his idea, a gift prepared for us in Jesus long before we knew anything about it. But we know it now. Since the appearance of our Savior, nothing could be plainer: death defeated, life vindicated in a steady blaze of light, all through the work of Jesus. (2 Timothy 8–10)

It's important that a church leader, responsible for the affairs in God's house, be looked up to— not pushy, not short-tempered, not a drunk, not a bully, not money-hungry. He must welcome people, be helpful, wise, fair, reverent, have a good grip on himself, and have a good grip on the Message, knowing how to use the truth to either spur people on in knowledge or stop them in their tracks if they oppose it. For there are a lot of rebels out there, full of loose, confusing, and deceiving talk. Those who were brought up religious and ought to know better are the worst. They've got to be shut up. They're disrupting entire families with their teaching, and all for the sake of a fast buck... Everything is clean to the clean-minded; nothing is clean to dirty-minded unbelievers. They leave their dirty fingerprints on every thought and act. They say they know God, but their actions speak louder than their words. They're real creeps, disobedient good-for-nothings. (Titus 1:7–11, 15–16)

I keep hearing of the love and faith you have for the Master Jesus, which brims over to other Christians. And I keep praying that this faith we hold in common keeps showing up in the good things we do, and that people recognize Christ in all of it. Friend, you have no idea how good your love makes me feel, doubly so when I see your hospitality to fellow believers. (Philemon 1:5–7)

Each time Paul came to a new location, he took the time to establish a relationship with the town's people. In each of his letters' opening lines, Paul establishes how the people's worldviews are influencing those around them. Those followers of Christ who are growing in the faith exhibit this in their actions and beliefs. Paul doesn't mention large church buildings, singular preachers, or great worship bands; he mentions their core actions and beliefs. The new Christian worldview changes the way people live, the way they act, and the way they are transforming the culture around them. It isn't always easy—and there isn't always a clear-cut plan—but God is changing the culture from the inside out.

Michael Frost, in *Exiles*, uses the acronym BELLS as a guide point to how we can have a follower-of-Jesus type of impact on the community around us.

B = Bless. This can take many forms and may be hard to do at first. Once you start blessing the people around you, however, your community grows in encouragement, support for one another, and overall consideration. Try doing one of these everyday:

- Send an email.
- Write on other people's Facebook walls.
- Send them tweets (the act of writing on Twitter).
- Send care packages.
- Shovel someone's driveway or mow a lawn.
- Just say "Thank you."

E = Eat. "We will eat with other members of our community at least three times each week."[167]

---

[167] Frost, Michael. *Exiles: Living Missionally in a Post-Christian Culture* (Peabody, MA: Hendrickson Publishers, 2006), p. 150.

- We eat together on Sundays.
- We should schedule breakfast meetings.
- And then at least one more time throughout the week.

L= Listen. "We will commit ourselves weekly to listening to the promptings of God in our lives."[168]

L = Learn. "We will read from the Gospels each week and remain diligent in learning more about Jesus."[169]

S = Sent. We will see our daily life as an expression of our calling to be stewards of creation by God, who sends us out into the world. "We are committed to looking out for ways in which our daily lives can be expressions of our 'sent-ness,' our mission as agents of God's grace on this planet."[170] We can do this by:

- Speaking truth into the lives of our communities.
- Engaging the marginalized people of our communities.
- Donating time or money to a cause within our communities.

Living a life in line with being a follower of Jesus, based on the BELLS acronym, leads us into a life that looks more like the New Testament church than the church of the twenty-first century. It's time for us to start thinking and

---

[168] Ibid.

[169] Ibid., p. 151.

[170] Ibid.

acting like the New Testament church. They started a revolution based on a new worldview. They stood out against the norm and said, "I want something more. I want a life that is everlasting."

Erwin McManus, in *The Barbarian Way*, explains quite simply why we need to become involved in communities at the most basic level, establishing the actions and beliefs of Christ as supreme.

> One of the tragedies of a civilized society is that no one wants to get involved. What becomes appropriate is to mind our own business. When we join a community that lacks a passionate heart for the world, we soon find ourselves acquiescing to apathy. It is a painful tragedy to see a brand-new follower of Christ alive with a barbarian spirit soon confirmed to the status quo.[171]

Joining God in his restoration process is to live out a new worldview that mirrors Christ's values.

A New Worldview

Rob Bell says, in his *Trees* Nooma video, that we live between two trees. The two trees he is referring to are found in Genesis 2:9 and Revelation 22:2:

> Then God planted a garden in Eden, in the east. He put the Man he had just made in it. God

---

[171] McManus, Erwin Raphael. *The Barbarian Way: Unleash the Untamed Faith Within* (Nashville, TN: Nelson Books, 2005), p. 123.

> made all kinds of trees grow from the ground,
> trees beautiful to look at and good to eat. The
> Tree-of-Life was in the middle of the garden,
> also the Tree-of-Knowledge-of-Good-and-Evil.
> (Genesis 2:9)

> It flowed from the Throne of God and the Lamb,
> right down the middle of the street. The Tree of
> Life was planted on each side of the River,
> producing twelve kinds of fruit, a ripe fruit each
> month. The leaves of the Tree are for healing the
> nations. (Revelation 22:2)

The question we then need to ask ourselves sounds something like this: what does this mean for us and our calling to a new worldview?

The answer is found when we live like we have a God that is alive today. When we live out a worldview that mirrors Christ, we are living a proclamation that God is still active, God is still in control, and God still guides our lives each and every day.

> I need a God that is now. I need a God who
> teaches me how to live now. I need a faith that's
> about today, which helps me understand the
> world that I live in today, the world that you and
> I know is here and now, the place Earth that we
> call home. I need to know how to live here and
> find meaning and purpose today.[172]

Worldviews are interesting because they establish a life that is full of purpose. When we live with a purpose, it calls

---

[172] Bell, Rob. *Discussion Guide 001* (Grand Rapids, MI: Zondervan, 2009), p. 62.

us into action, off the sidelines, and into a life working with
God, promoting his values.

> We live between the trees in a world drenched
> in God. And some people seriously ask, "Where
> is God?" Maybe a better question would be,
> "Where isn't God?" I mean, his fingerprints are all
> over our world. Or maybe it's his world, and
> they're our fingerprints.[173]

Rob Bell asks some very important questions in that
statement that I think we should all wrestle and challenge
ourselves with. But I think there is a deeper, more
important question that we need to ask ourselves: in what
ways are we putting our fingerprints on his world?

The answer should come to us through a biblical
worldview that establishes our actions, which in the end
maintain and present our beliefs to the world.

We are given some clear examples throughout the Bible
of how we can strengthen our faith, maintain our biblical
worldview, and grow our personal relationship with God.
These examples are called spiritual disciplines. Discipline is a
good word for these practices and I won't sugar-coat it—
they are difficult, just like any other life change we try to
make. It takes time and energy to make significant changes
in our lives, but by adding spiritual discipline we can grow
closer to God.

As we jump into these spiritual disciplines, we need to
address a couple of things.

---

[173] Ibid.

- As a leader: How do we even begin to teach our kids these basic, foundational truths?
- As a Christian: Are our kids part of our lives? So many times, ministries become more about what we do than who we are. We become youth workers and youth pastors. It sometimes becomes hard to read the Bible just for content. I really struggle with this one. I find it hard to read the Bible, a book, or a newspaper without consistently emailing myself quotes, stats, and other information I can use for my talks. I sometimes wish I could just *be* with God and not have this thought process always going on.

Silence and Solitude

Silence is a temporary abstinence from speaking so that other spiritual goals can be attained. If you are like me, you wake up to music, take a couple steps into the shower, and turn on a radio. Then you walk downstairs and turn on phones, computers, and the TV. If you are like me, you medicate yourself all day with noise.

Why?

For many of us, this idea of being silent, on purpose, for any length of time, is frightening. When we turn off the noise, we have to deal with things like shame, loneliness, and the many shortcomings of life. It is a terrifying concept for us. Dallas Willard said in the book, *Spirit of the Disciplines,* that "silence is frightening because it strips us as nothing else does, throwing us upon the stark realities of our life."[174] In the silence, you cannot hide. We are confronted with our emptiness, loneliness, shortfalls, and regrets. So why would anyone want to spend time in silence if it leads us to confront these negative feelings?

The reason is simple. Jesus called us to fellowship, but how can we have a relationship with him if we don't spend time alone with him?

How does silence allow us to achieve other spiritual goals?

The time we spend in silence allows us to read clearly, speak openly, and listen attentively to the still, small quiet voice of God. It is through outward silence that we can begin to ask ourselves some very tough questions.

Do we fit God into our busy lives or do we expect him to find a place within our daily schedules?

Spending time in silence will in turn lead us into times of solitude. Finding silence and finding solitude are two complementary disciplines. Together, they allow us to spend some very important alone time with God. Solitude is the voluntary removal from all things public so that we can again, like with silence, be in God's presence. The hard part is finding a way to balance the busyness of our lives with our calling to create a relationship with God. "Without silence and solitude we're shallow, without fellowship we're stagnant. Balance requires them all."[175]

Time spent in silence and solitude creates within us an understanding of our true selves. It allows us to get in touch

---

[174] Willard, Dallas. *The Spirit of the Disciplines* (San Francisco, CA: Harper & Row, 1988), p. 163.
[175] Whitney, Donald S. *Spiritual Disciplines for the Christian Life* (Colorado Springs, CO: NavPress, 1991), p. 184.

with our hearts, speak what is on our minds, and listen to the very plans God has for us. If we don't spend this time alone with God, our understanding of who we are becomes based on what the world tells us. Silence and solitude allows our understanding of who we are to be based on what God has created us to be.

Stephen Neil explains the connection between fellowship and solitude by saying,

> Modern man is a little afraid of being alone and of being still... Because we are afraid to know ourselves, we find difficulty in knowing one another. Because we do not know how to withdraw into ourselves, we find it hard fully to go out to other people.[176]

Our discomfort with silence and solitude is that their essence goes against everything the world tells us. Silence and solitude may not be the world's way of living, but they are Jesus' way.

Not sure that Jesus teaches this way? Check out these passages from his words:

> LAMENTATIONS 3:28–29, HABAKKUK 2:20, LUKE 6:12–13, JAMES 1:19, MATTHEW 4:1, PSALMS 46:10, MATTHEW 14:13, PSALMS 19:14, MATTHEW 14:23, JOB 2:13, GENESIS 24:63, MARK 6:31, MARK 1:34, PSALMS 62:1–2, 5–6, LUKE 1:20, GALATIANS 1:17, LUKE 5:16,

---

[176] Ford, Leighton. *Transforming Leadership: Jesus' Way of Creating Vision, Shaping Values & Empowering Change* (Downers Grove, IL: InterVarsity Press, 1991), p. 129.

ZECHARIAH 2:13, 1 KINGS 19:11–13, PSALMS
77:12, JOB 29:21, ZEPHANIAH 1:7, HABAKKUK
2:1, LUKE 4:42, AND ECCLESIASTES 3:7.

In some instances, the Holy Spirit guides Jesus into
times of solitude and silence so that the very worldly
treasures that tempt us could tempt him. In Luke 4, we read
that the Spirit guided Jesus out into the desert, where he
was tempted by the devil. *"Now Jesus, full of the Holy Spirit,
left the Jordan and was led by the Spirit into the wild"* (Luke
4:1). Jesus, at that very moment, had to wrestle with being
alone and being offered the whole world. Jesus beat the
temptation: *"Jesus returned to Galilee powerful in the Spirit.
News that he was back spread through the countryside"* (Luke
4:14).

Many times, Scripture points out that through times of
silence and solitude lives are transformed. Jesus understood
that a balance was required between our busy, noisy,
everyday lives and the stillness that silence and solitude
brings. The question we always ask is, how far away from
God can I get and still be a Christian? We should really be
asking how and where we can listen to God and get closer.
Jesus said it plain as day in Philippians 4:9: *"Whatever you
have learned or received or heard from me, or seen in me—put into
practice. And the God of peace will be with you"* (NIV).

Have a look at what the Old Testament teaches about
the benefits of purposeful silence. 1 Kings 19:12–13
establishes that in silence we can hear from God. Elijah
hears God not in the raging winds or violent earthquake but
in a still, small voice:

And after the earthquake a fire, but the Lord was
not in the fire; and after the fire a sound of sheer
silence. When Elijah heard it, he wrapped his
face in his mantle and went out and stood at the
entrance of the cave. Then there came a voice to
him that said, "What are you doing here, Elijah?"
(1 Kings 19:12–13, NRSV)

Where are you searching for God's guidance?

God proves to be good to the man who
passionately waits, to the woman who diligently
seeks. It's a good thing to quietly hope, quietly
hope for help from God. It's a good thing when
you're young to stick it out through the hard
times. When life is heavy and hard to take, go off
by yourself. Enter the silence. (Lamentations
3:25–28)

Does patience come easily to you?

It is in the words of Habakkuk, the prophet, where we
find the hardest concept for us to grasp when it comes to
purposeful silence. Silence is used to worship God. *"But oh!
God is in his holy Temple! Quiet everyone—a holy silence.
Listen!"* (Habakkuk 2:20) I wonder if in silence, true silence,
we hear from God because it is at that point where we shut
out everything around us and hear only what he intends for
us to hear. In that moment, are we like Elijah on the
mountain as we hear only a still, small sound?

We have become so used to all the noise around us that
we expect God to speak to us in the same way. We shout to
get people's attention; it is how we rise up over all that is
around us. When we become louder, we are looking to

make a connection with someone who cannot hear us, but God works differently.

> There was silence before God spoke the world into existence, and silence for forty days before Jesus began His public ministry, which may indicate that silence is what allows us to speak as God intends.[177]

The words of Psalms 46:10 provide the connection point between our silence and our understanding of God. Silence becomes our link in establishing lines of communication with God.

> If I am not silent, and if I don't listen, how is Jesus going to give me rest?... Have you spent the same amount of time worrying and talking about your difficult, confusing situations as you have spent in silence, listening to what God might have to say?[178]

Silence is not just about receiving secret messages from God. It is about gaining truth and insights from the word of God. Charles R. Swindoll breaks down silence that way in his book, *So, You Want to Be Like Christ?*

> Yet somehow in the crucible of silence the Holy Spirit boils the truth we receive from Scripture down to its essence, reveals specific insights that are pertinent, and then applies them to our most

---

[177] Driscoll, Mark. "Silence," *The Resurgence*, http://theresurgence.com/silence (accessed March 8, 2010).
[178] *Nooma: 005 Noise*, DVD, 2003.

perplexing problems and our most stubborn
misconceptions. As He transforms our heart to
beat more truly for Him, our decisions
accomplish His will as we reflect His character.[179]

The companion to silence is solitude. They are companions because time spent in solitude, although frightening and nerve-wracking for most of us, provides key moments of reflection so that we can keep our worldview and God's word on the same page. However, getting time alone can be difficult, but let's take some more words from Charles Swindoll:

> Don't fight it. Don't rush it. And don't feel guilty.
> It's normal. Just let your mind run. Eventually,
> without trying and before you know it, your
> mind is still. Not empty; just quiet. And the things
> you have studied, the lessons you have learned,
> the scripture you have read or memorized, the
> prayers you have begun to pray will start to
> mingle and finally jell. The silly will be displaced
> by meaningful thoughts. Shallow will disappear
> as depth finds its way in.[180]

Solitude and silence bring us closer to God because it is in those times when we say "No" to distractions—whether it is TV, the Internet, friends, or even voices around us. We do, however, say "Yes" to his will and his word. God meets us in our silence and solitude and takes those fears of being

---

[179] Swindoll, Charles R. *So, You Want to Be Like Christ?: Eight Essentials to Get You There* (Nashville, TN: W. Pub. Group, 2005), p. 63.
[180] Ibid., p. 71.

alone and places them in his hands as he embraces us as friends.

I often struggle with connecting my ancient faith with my modern world. That is a statement I find myself repeating every time I get up to speak to groups of people. Spiritual disciplines are an essential piece to the puzzle. Solitude and silence allow us to connect with God by making it easier for us to hear his voice, but sacrificial and simple living connects us to the very way Jesus lived.

We live in a culture of stuff. Quantity often takes the place of quality and we get caught up in the earthly desires all around us. God's word tells us over and over again that simple and sacrificial living is, in essence, living with compassion.

Here are some helpful hints for practicing silence and solitude:

- It's okay to be on your own.
- Turn off your cell phone and media devices for a designated amount of time every day.
- Spend some time with God in prayer every day.
- Journal every day.

And now for some resources:

- Nooma 005: Noise
- *TED Talk: The Power of Time Off*, by Stephen Sagmeister (http://www.ted.com/talks/stefan_sagmeister_th e_power_of_time_off.html)

- *Spiritual Disciplines for the Christian Life*, by Donald S. Whitney (Colorado Springs, CO: NavPress, 1991)
- The *Developing HABITS* curriculum, from Simply Youth.
- *The Spirit of the Disciplines*, by Dallas Willard (San Francisco, CA: HarperSanFrancisco, 1990)
- *The Way of the Heart*, by Henri Nouwen (New York, NY: Ballantine Books, 1991)
- *Celebration of Discipline: The Path To Spiritual Growth*, by Richard Foster (San Francisco, CA: Harper & Row, 1978)

Simple and Sacrificial Living

I'll never forget the time I spent in Guatemala on a mission's team with my church working with Doctors Without Borders. All I did was mix cement. If you've seen *Slumdog Millionaire*, you know what it was like in the city dump where I was working. 25,000-30,000 people lived in that dump.

With me was a nine-year-old boy. Both of his parents were dead, he couldn't read or write, and he had never been to school a day in his life. He lived alone in the dump. We were working with him and he was mixing cement with me.

After a few weeks, I said to him that we were going to take him out to Burger King. If you have ever been to

Guatemala, it is a little strange—death, destruction, and...
Burger King.

He looked at me and said, with the aid of an interpreter,
"I had Burger King the other week."

I asked a question at that point that I thought was really
normal: "Who took you?"

Right. Someone takes you to Burger King. That is
normal to us. We go with friends to fast food restaurants,
but what happened next I will never forget.

He turned and looked at me like I was nuts. "Brett, no
one took me. I was the first to the garbage truck, I grabbed
the bag and went off to the side..." I started to feel sick,
because I knew where this is going. "...I ripped it open and
inside was Burger King."

I began to cry. Honestly, this kid was about nine years
old and his first burger was out of a garbage bag that
someone threw away.

What's your biggest problem today? Think about it.

Well, I'll tell you mine. It's the pain in my elbow from
working out. It's wondering what I'm going to have for
dinner tonight and whether or not I will clean my office
and garage. Those are my biggest issues in the world. Most
of the issues running through our heads right now have to
do with affluence.

Your car.

Your vacation.

Your home.

Where is your heart? Is it in money? Clothes? CDs,
DVDs, or MP3s?

Or is your heart focused on God?

"For where your treasure is, there your heart will be also" (Matthew 6:21, NIV).

Have you ever watched those new reality shows that deal with money and debt? The TV show '*Til Debt Do Us Part* is one of those shows. *Til Debt Do Us Part* follows financial guru Gail Vaz-Oxlade and her interactions with families as she tries to get to the root of their spending habits.

> Money is the number one cause of failed marriages. Rare is the couple that agrees on how the pot should be divided and the bills paid. Most families are in debt, and with debt come family arguments, tears, tantrums and marriages on the verge of divorce. To save families from the doldrums of debt...[181]

If I were to follow you around just like Gail does for a week, I would be able to tell you where your heart is.

God's word is full of warnings based on the love of money and earthly desires.

> Two-thirds of Jesus' parables spoke directly about money or passions. In the gospels, one of every ten verses addresses financial issues. In all of Scripture, over 2300 verses talk about money.[182]

---

[181] Slice, "Til Debt Do Us Part," *Slice*, http://www.slice.ca/shows/showspage.aspx?title_id=93097 (accessed August 2, 2010).
[182] Groeschel, Craig. *Chazown: A Different Way to See Your Life* (Sisters, OR: Multnomah Publishers, 2006), p. 154.

Still not sure about what God tells us about simple and sacrificial living? Then check out these verses:

> DEUTERONOMY 8:18, JAMES 4:1–2, MATTHEW 10:21–27, MARK 4:18–19, PROVERBS 11:4, PSALMS 37:16, LUKE 6:30, PROVERBS 23:4–5, LEVITICUS 25:23, 1 TIMOTHY 6:8–10, ACTS 4:34–35, LUKE 16:19–31, LUKE 12:29–34, PROVERBS 30:8–9, PSALMS 37:7, PROVERBS 28:20, 1 JOHN 3:16–18, REVELATION 3:17–19, LUKE 12:47–48, MATTHEW 6:19–21, MATTHEW 6:33, 1 TIMOTHY 6:5, LUKE 14:33, ECCLESIASTES 5:10–15, 1 TIMOTHY 6:17–19, PROVERBS 3:9, MATTHEW 6:24, PSALMS 49:16–19, MATTHEW 23:23, ACTS 2:44–45, HEBREWS 3:5, LUKE 12:33–34, PHILIPPIANS 4:11–13, JEREMIAH 9:23–24, JOB 31:24–25, LUKE 16:9–11, 2 CORINTHIANS 2:17, LUKE 8:14, AND 1 THESSALONIANS 2:5.

There is a great challenge in Richard Foster's book, *Freedom of Simplicity*. It goes like this: "Stop trying to impress people with your clothes and impress them with your life."[183] I think many of us fall into this trap.

Do we find it easier to talk to our friends about the new clothes we bought over the weekend than what we learned at church? Do we define ourselves more by the very brands we put on our backs than by our actions every day?

Our love of brands and possessions make true compassion very difficult.

---

[183] Foster, Richard J. *Freedom of Simplicity* (San Francisco, CA: Harper San Francisco, 2005), p. 158.

> We can't reach far enough to offer compassion
> because our arms are too busy holding all what
> we own. If, on the other hand, we recognize that
> what we have is a gift, then we can extend our
> reach. We discover that we can use a portion of
> our gift to improve someone else's life, maybe
> even to save someone else's life.[184]

This is a good start to figuring out our problem with simple and sacrificial giving, but I think it goes deeper than just having too much. I think it comes down to not having enough love and compassion. We have a hard time connecting with those who are hurting or have lost everything, because we are used to having all the "things" in our lives that make us feel secure. All the iPods, BlackBerrys, Starbucks, and having enough in our cupboards to last for months have taken away our ability to connect or feel compassion for those who are lacking. Feelings of entitlement have replaced feelings of compassion and we can no longer relate to those on the streets. We are so used to having everything that having nothing is something we cannot comprehend.

Have we become used to seeing people lying in the streets as we walk to school, work, or home?

Has it gotten to the point that the problem seems too big to fix?

If we are going to be Christ-like, should we not love our neighbour and be moved to show compassion for those

---

[184] Davis, Tom. *Red Letters: Living a Faith that Bleeds* (Colorado Springs, CO: David C. Cook, 2007), p. 39.

who are cold and hungry? Is their pain not large enough to move us to action?

We won't understand simple, sacrificial giving until we start truly giving what we do not have.

How do we do that?

We start by giving beyond our surplus. What I mean by that is that we give not because we have some money left over at the end of the week—after we have bought everything else that we thought we needed. Mother Teresa said it best:

> I hope you are not giving only your surplus. You need to give what costs you, make a sacrifice, go without something you like, that your gift may have some value before God. Then you will be truly brothers and sisters to the poor who are deprived of even the things they need.[185]

Can you go without your tall soy chai latte everyday?

Do you really need McDonald's twice a week? However, it needs to go deeper. Simple, sacrificial giving is all about understanding and practicing compassion. It is impossible to separate Christ and compassion; they are seamlessly braided together.[186] Paul explains it very clearly in Philippians 3:10. To be like Christ, he says, is to want to transform our whole life to reflect him. *"I gave up all that inferior stuff so I could know Christ personally, experience his resurrection power, be a partner in his suffering, and go all the way*

---

[185] Mother Teresa. *The Revolution: A Field Manual for Changing Your World* (Orlando, FL: Relevant Books, 2006), p. XIII.
[186] Rick Warren, Leadership Summit at Willow Creek Community Church in Chicago, August 2006.

with him to death itself." Actually, all of Philippians 3 is about transforming our lives to be like Christ and continually striving to achieve it.

Did you catch the key to Paul's words? *"Be a partner in his suffering, and go all the way with him to death itself."* To be like Christ is to practice sacrificial living. Is that not what Jesus did on the cross? *"This is how much God loved the world: He gave his Son, his one and only Son. And this is why: so that no one need be destroyed; by believing in him, anyone can have a whole and lasting life"* (John 3:16). Paul tells us that this type of living is needed:

> Watch what God does, and then you do it, like children who learn proper behavior from their parents. Mostly what God does is love you. Keep company with him and learn a life of love. Observe how Christ loved us. His love was not cautious but extravagant. He didn't love in order to get something from us but to give everything of himself to us. Love like that. (Ephesians 5:1–2)

Sacrifice is a deep commitment to being like Christ. It screams out trust and love to our Saviour. The definition of sacrifice is to give up something for the sake of something greater.

> Personal sacrifice begins with choice; who will we trust to meet our needs? We naturally serve what we trust. Hoarding wealth is a sure sign that a person trusts his things instead of his God.[187]

---

[187] Swindoll, Charles R. *So, You Want to Be Like Christ?: Eight Essentials to Get You There* (Nashville, TN: W. Pub. Group, 2005), p. 177.

Let's go back to the verse in Matthew: *"For where your treasure is, there your heart will be also"* (Matthew 6:21, NIV).

Where is your heart? Sometimes we don't give because we are stuck asking ourselves questions like, "How will I manage...?" When we are stuck on questions like this, are we really trusting God to provide for us? *"Look at the birds. They don't plant or harvest or store food in barns, for your heavenly Father feeds them. And aren't you far more valuable to him than they are?"* (Matthew 6:26, NLT)

The practice of simple, sacrificial living can start small— real small. Start by donating the coffee money you think you so desperately need to get through those long, cold February mornings. Those mornings may be cold for you, even though we have perfectly fine winter wear from North Face, but what about the morning for the homeless man lying on the corner who you pass every day on your way to school? Do you not think the morning is particularly cold and painful for them?

Here is a practical test in simple and sacrificial living. Start with a blank piece of paper, like the one on the next page.

Now write out everything you have done with your money. Try looking back a year; that way, you will have a better understanding of where you have been placing your priorities. If you cannot remember back that far, I think the answer to where your money is going is—nowhere.

What does your list look like? Okay, now take off everything on the list which you bought for your friends and family.

If I asked you to take away all the things you put on your list that were for you, would there be anything left?

Practical Test: Simple and Sacrificial Living

If simple, sacrificial living is living like Christ through loving actions and compassionate hearts towards others by giving up something for something greater, then the next step should not be too difficult. Having the ability to serve is a key step towards living like Christ. *"Whatever you do, whether in word or deed, do it all in the name of the Lord Jesus, giving thanks to God the Father through him"* (Colossians 3:17, NIV). Again, we need to notice that our actions, and how we live our everyday lives, are of key importance if we are to be agents of transformation in this world.

Our church has recently signed on to www.thecommon.org. TheCommon.org believes that people want to get involved but don't know where to look.

> We believe people want to help each other, but the challenge is making the need known and finding the right people to respond. TheCommon.org provides real-time connectivity for members of a community to share their needs and abilities—opportunities to get and give help—and to build stronger communities in the process. It's connecting with a purpose.[188]

You sign up as a church, then log in and say what you can help with—or what you need help with. The program matches the requests to get things done. Emails are sent to your phones or home computers.

---

[188] TheCommon.org. "More Info," www.thecommon.org/home/more_info (accessed January 26, 2011).

This is just one practical way to become involved with your community and donate your time and skills to someone that needs it.

We live like the kings and queens of England we laugh at on shows like *The Tudors*. We live in our own world of affluence. We have changed summer homes and castles into cottages at the lake. We have multiple cars, our lives resolve around vacations, and all we talk about is entertainment. Entertainment has taken over our lives in a time when God calls us to live sacrificially.

This doesn't mean that we need to sell all our possessions or that we cannot buy the car we've always dreamed of, but it's about time we questioned the financial decisions we make everyday. How can we use what God has blessed us with to help the world around us?

The following verses describe what should motivate us to serve. They provide examples of serving, as well as some application tips.

> HEBREWS 9:14, PSALMS 100:2, DEUTERONOMY 13:4, 1 SAMUEL 12:24, NEHEMIAH 2:2–6, ISAIAH 6:6–8, JOHN 13:12–16, PHILIPPIANS 2:3, GALATIANS 5:13, 2 CORINTHIANS 5:14–15, MARK 12:28–31, 1 CORINTHIANS 12:4,11, 1 PETER 4:10, EPHESIANS 4:12, ROMANS 1:1, COLOSSIANS 1:29, 1 CORINTHIANS 15:58, HEBREWS 6:10, JOSHUA 24:15, LUKE 22:27, MARK 9: 33–35, 1 JOHN 3:18, MATTHEW 20:20–28, PHILIPPIANS 2:5–11, ACTS 9:36, AND ROMANS 16:1.

Here are some practical ideas you can use for living sacrificial lives:

- Find a cause that you believe in and start donating to it.
- Make financial plans.
- Declutter your life by donating the stuff you don't need or use.
- Give back to your church.
- Give to local charities that touch your heart and which you feel led to give to.

And now some resources:

- *Beyond Me: Living a You-First Life in a Me-First World*, by Kathi Macias (Birmingham, AL: New Hope, 2008)
- *Holy Discontent*, by Bill Hybels (Grand Rapids, MI: Zondervan, 2008)
- *Irresistible Revolution*, by Shane Claiborne (Grand Rapids, MI: Zondervan, 2007)
- *Starving Jesus*, by Craig Gross (Colorado Springs, CO: David C. Cook, 2007)
- *Deep Justice: Journeys*, a learning curriculum from Youth Specialties
- *Freedom of Simplicity*, by Richard J. Foster (San Francisco, CA: Harper & Row, 1981)
- *The Radical Disciple*, by John Stott (Nottingham, UK: InterVarsity, 2010)

- www.thecommon.org
- *Under the Overpass: A Journey of Faith on the Streets of America*, by Mike Yankoski (Sisters, OR: Multnomah, 2010)
- *The Challenge of the Disciplined Life*, by Richard Foster (London, UK: Hodder Christian, 2005)

Service

Christ describes the church as a body that needs to work together in order to make any change or growth possible. Without the cooperative nature of a group of individuals, life becomes like a three-legged race where we forcefully drag our partner towards the finish line with little success. Until we realize that we are not the center of the universe or the star of the story, or until we drop our pride, we will be unable to serve with a servant's heart.

> The church is not here for us. We are the church, and we are here for the world. When I ask church people to serve somewhere, I often receive a polite, "I'll pray about it, Pastor." (Which generally means, "Oh, crap. I don't want to do that, but I'll say something spiritual that may buy me time to plan my excuse.")[189]

I have worked with many youth pastors who have told me stories just like this. They tell me of 30-Hour Famine events where their youth have declined to fundraise or

---

[189] Groeschel, Graig. *Confessions of a Pastor* (Sisters , OR: Multnomah Publishers, 2006), p. 34.

attend because they do not want to go thirty hours without food. The event, at that point, becomes all about them and how hungry they will be throughout the night. They forget something—that they are part of a larger story.

Our churches should be involved with every community event that takes place, simply because we have experience with exactly the sorts of activities that happen at community events.

Let's look at some examples for a minute. Have you ever been to a community event and witnessed a person working with a group of forty kids, a person who looks like they're about to go into shock from not being able to handle them? Ask yourself how many kids go through your church every week and how well the children's and youth ministries handle it. They're prepared for the numbers and for the fun that comes with what most see just as chaos. How about parking cars? Most large churches have parking attendants who could be of great service at community events.

It's about time we got out and involved ourselves with community activities. We need to start being the hands and feet that God calls us to be in our communities. If we do, the church will slowly become more than the building on the corner.

My wife, Dawn, decided to make a difference after university, so she joined up with an organization called The Mercy Ships (www.mercyships.org). The Mercy Ships are floating hospitals. She travelled up and down the Ivory Coast of West Africa, helping people she didn't know. I met my wife and fell in love not only with her but with the things she loves, like The Mercy Ships. We place money aside every year for that organization because we believe in what they're doing in the world.

What do you believe in?

People always have an answer to that question. Whether it's AIDS, diabetes, or fresh water, everyone has something that matters to them. It never fails that someone will say breast cancer. My aunt died because of breast cancer, so it occupies a place of value within my own heart.

When someone tells me what they care about, I say, "Prove it."

Is there anyone not against breast cancer? How about AIDS? Is there anyone not against famine? We are all against those things. My point is this: are you against it only by words, or by heart and action? Have you ever been part of a foundation's fundraising effort, like a bike marathon or something to that effect? Have you given money? I'm not talking about the lottery ticket draws; I'm taking about sacrificial giving. When I ask these questions, a lot of people look at me and have no response. It seems like they're only in it for talk; they're not willing to get involved with their hands and feet.

How about we start giving biblically to the church? When a pastor goes to the front of the church and asks for money, it becomes everyone's issue. When the average person gives only two percent of his or her annual income back to the church, we have a problem. How do we know that there's a problem? When our entertainment budgets, vacation plans, and car lease payments are larger than what we give the church, we have heart issues. Our budgets show what we value.

How about we get involved with things outside the church as well? We give to the church weekly, but that doesn't mean we cannot look outside the church for opportunities. When you get some extra cash, try praying to God, asking, "God, what can I do with this money?"

I once challenged the members of a youth group to each donate twenty bucks and have a shopping event that wasn't about them. So they did. They each took their money and went to a grocery store en masse. I would have loved to have been there as one hundred students showed up at once, depleting the store's stock in a matter of a couple of hours. They came out with bags and boxes of groceries to give away.

We all know that young people don't always do things in a logical manner. They didn't just knock on people's doors, hand out the food, and say "God bless!" They packed them on the roofs of people's cars, in their trees, on their lawns, then knocked on the door and ran away screaming. In one case, a man and woman walked out of their house and started to cry when they witnessed the generosity and service of love these young people had blessed their lives with.

What is God saying to us about money? How about we get involved biblically?

> What you'll get is the Holy Spirit. And when the
> Holy Spirit comes on you, you will be able to be

my witnesses in Jerusalem, all over Judea and
Samaria, even to the ends of the world. (Acts 1:8)

Jerusalem, Judea, Samaria, and the ends of the world. This verse isn't telling us to stay local first, then go global; it tells us to go everywhere! We are to take the actions of Jesus to *all* of these places. What are you doing locally, provincially, nationally, and internationally?

Here are a few examples for you. Locally, go to the schools and ask if they have reading programs. I would love to see students donating their time to read to younger students on a weekly basis, especially to those kids who wake up every day without a father or mother. Think of how much good our groups could do if they simply sat down and read to kids at our local libraries. Those kids who don't have a dad might finally know the feeling of having an older male read stories to them. The same goes for the girls who don't have mothers. Through such an act, you could change someone's world forever.

You can help out with food banks. Food banks are popping up in almost every community that desperately need assistance. In Toronto, we have Urban Promise, an organization through which you can sponsor a teenager from a variety of rough neighbourhoods. It only costs thirty dollars per month, or a dollar per day.

I have had World Vision and Compassion kids on my fridge since before I can remember. It doesn't matter what organization you go through, sponsoring a child is one of the easiest ways you can demonstrate that everything isn't about you.

From there, move out and look at AIDS, famine, the sex trade, slavery, and child soldiers in Uganda and other parts of the world. Do you realize that there is more slavery today than at any other point in the history of mankind?

A guy once put up his hand and said, "Brett, what about Barack Obama?"

"What?!" I replied.

"What about Barack Obama?" the guy repeated.

"Dude, do you think that upwards of two hundred million slaves just disappeared because of the election of an African American president? What kind of stupid question is that?"

I have never seen someone sit down so fast in my life.

Honestly, we live in a bubble in North America, a bubble where we think that *our* world is *the* world. It is not. At this very moment, I can go and buy a kid for twelve bucks.[190] I can buy a person's life for twelve bucks! Think about the fact that there is a child out there who's just like your child, trying to have the same childhood experiences, but you could buy his or her life and change it forever.

The sad thing is that they are being bought for the sex trade. Their lives can be drastically turned upside-down for the same cost as today's lunch. We are the privileged, and with privilege comes responsibility. We have to start taking action and responsibility for the world we live in and show that Christ's redemptive, healing, and restoring nature is still at work. As the privileged, it's our responsibility to make a change in the lives of those who need our help.

---

[190] Hays, Jeffery. "Prostitution and Hostess Bars in China," http://factsanddetails.com/index.php?itemid=1002 (accessed April 2, 2011).

Louie Giglio, a terrific and gifted speaker, takes the time in the book, *I Know I Am Not But I Know I Am,* to describe what it means to admit that we are not the star of this story:

> But to mean it when I say that I want my life to count for His glory is to drive a stake through the heart of self—a painful and determined dying to me that must be a part of every day that I live... Humility, another word for knowing my name is I am not, can be described as "seeing God as He is." Pride is simply an admission that I haven't seen God at all.[191]

Service towards others requires pride to be placed in check, so that we can show and mirror the very life of Christ. Events like the 30-Hour Famine are not for ourselves; sure, they are fun and exciting times, but they are meant to benefit others. "The church does not exist for the benefit of its members. It exists to equip its members for the benefit of the world."[192] The famine event is just one example of ways in which we can benefit the world through our actions. It is a gruelling thirty hours because we are not used to being without food that long.

Can you imagine what it would be like to go three days without food?

That is only one question, but what about these questions from Bill Hybels in *Holy Disconnect*?

---

[191] Giglio, Louie. *I Am Not, But I Know I Am* (Sisters, OR: Multnomah Publishers, 2005), pp. 128–129.
[192] McLaren, Brian. *A New Kind of Christian: A Tale of Two Friends on a Spiritual Journey* (San Francisco, CA: Jossey-Bass, 2001), p. 155.

> What about the poor? Who will care for the sick
> and the dying? Will anyone visit the prisoners?
> Who will clothe the naked? Or take in orphans?
> Or listen to the hurting? Or give water to the
> thirsty, food to the hungry, and community to
> the outcast?[193]

What is that one thing in the world that when you think about it, it hurts? It wrecks you emotionally; it drives you to anger over the way things are. Take that one thing and strive to change it. Take that passion you feel and serve those who are stuck in those situations.

How many of you have been asked if the glass is half empty or half full? What if I told you there could be a third option?

> A pessimist, they say, sees a glass of water as
> being half-empty; and an optimist sees the glass
> as half-full. But a giving person sees a glass of
> water and starts looking for someone who might
> be thirsty.[194]

When we serve others, we are choosing to live out an active faith. A faith that shouts, "I will not sit back and accept a world that is out of whack." Dallas Willard, in *Spirits of Discipline*, explains the importance of serving as a retraction of negative qualities of life:

[193] Hybels, Bill. *Holy Disconnect: Fueling the Fire that Ignites Personal Vision* (Grand Rapids , MI: Zondervan, 2007), p. 61.
[194] Gale, Donald. *The Revolution : A Field Manual for Changing Your World* (Orlando, FL: Relevant Books, 2006), p. 1.

> I will often be able to serve another simply as an act of love and righteousness, without regard to how it may enhance my abilities to follow Christ. There certainly is nothing wrong with that, and it may, incidentally, strengthen me spiritually as well. But I may also serve another to train myself away from arrogance, possessiveness, envy, resentment, or covetousness. In that case, my service is undertaken as a discipline for the spiritual life.[195]

Service, at this point, moves beyond our pride, beyond our love of watching life and not taking part.

Practically, you might be asking, "How do I do this?" Well, try shoveling snow. It's a great way to get to know the people who live around you. You can help them cut their grass. Again, it's a great way to meet your neighbours. Try volunteering at soup kitchens, food banks, or single parent homes, blessing others through acts of service. Clean windows, feed the poor, paint a fence... just do whatever it takes to bless those who are in need. The only way soup kitchens and food banks can continue to do what they need to do is if they have the money to stay afloat. Single parents work so hard that they deserve a helping hand in times of need.

I hear this all the time from organizations all over Toronto: "Hey Brett, I'm so-and-so from such-and-such organization. We had a group come down to help us because of what you said at your talk the other night. It cost us one hundred dollars to make them feel good."

[195] Willard, Dallas. *The Spirit of the Disciplines* (San Francisco, CA: Harper & Row, 1988), p. 182.

I just cringe when I hear that. If we're going to go to these organizations to help out, we need to actually help out. Take twenty bucks each and go to Home Depot and buy the paint as a group, buy the cleaning supplies, or get a gift certificate and hand it to the organizations so that they can get what they need. We need to pay for everything, so that we can bless them.

Serving others is a way to grow spiritually as we leave behind our pride and take steps towards embracing Christ-like qualities. When we make the choice to serve in Christ-like fashion, we do so with humility, because it's impossible to serve as Christ served without humility.

Here are some practical ideas for service opportunities.

- Conduct a 30-Hour Famine, by World Vision.
- Have a movie night, with the proceeds going towards a good cause.
- Hold a service day for the members of your community.
- Serve locally in schools or with neighbours.
- Serve regionally through food banks and homeless shelters.
- Serve globally through clean water projects, sex trafficking, AIDS, or other global issues.
- Shovel snow in the winter and cut lawns in the summer.
- Invite your friends for dinner, even if they're non-Christians.

- Choose one organization for your youth group to support and raise funds for.

Here are some good resources you can look at:

- *Red Letters: Living a Life that Bleeds*, by Tom Davis (Colorado Springs, CO: David C. Cook, 2007)
- *The Search for God and Guinness*, by Stephen Mansfield (Nashville, TN: Thomas Nelson, 2009)
- www.thecommon.org

Worship

In the church, we are so blinded by the contemporary use of the term "worship." We take this term to literally mean nothing more than the corporate singing of praises to God.

What does worship mean to you?

A.W. Tozer describes the nature of worship as being a lifestyle and not an act at all:

> If you will not worship God seven days a week
> you do not worship him one day a week.
> Worship is not something that happens at a time
> and a place. Worship is a lifestyle that includes
> something that happens in a time and a place.[196]

---

[196] Tozer, A.W. *The Tozer Pulpit*, Vol. 1 (Camp Hill, PA: Christian Publications, 1994), p. 51.

There are many ways to worship God once we understand that singing is not the end of it. Think about some of these examples:

1. Loving others.
2. Missions.
3. Spiritual zealousness.
4. Hospitality.
5. Acts of service.
6. Charity towards unbelievers.
7. Sacrifice.
8. Work, career, vocation.
9. Seeking justice.
10. Exercising spiritual gifts.
11. Not conforming to societal norms.
12. Singing worship songs.
13. Giving tithes and offerings.

Worship comes down to focusing our minds and hearts towards God. "To worship God is to ascribe the proper worth to God, to magnify His worthiness of praise, or better, to approach and address God as He is worthy."[197] True worship means that you have your mind, body, heart, and soul all focused on the greatness of God. To be that focused on something takes more than words; it takes a complete life to ascribe that much greatness to something.

One family that used their life and work to worship God was the Guinness family. Yes, that is Guinness like the

[197] Whitney, Donald. S. *Spiritual Disciplines for the Christian Life* (Colorado Springs, CO: NavPress, 1991), p. 87.

beer, and yes, they started brewing beer and creating a company that showed value in actions and words. Stephen Mansfield, in a biographical look at the Guinness brand and family, discovered it was the family's lifestyle towards social justice issues that made the company what it is today.

> What distinguishes his story is that he understood his success as forming a kind of mandate, a kind of calling to a purpose of God beyond just himself and his family to the broader good he could do in the world.[198]

Arthur Guinness built his company through focusing his mind and heart towards the people of Dublin. They (the Guinness men) also knew that what they had was a blessing from God.

> The continued good account of our Business calls for much thankfulness to Almighty God while we humbly ask for the infinitely higher blessings of His grace in the Lord Jesus Christ...[199]

The Guinness men of faith took what they were good at, what they trained and apprenticed each other to do, and concluded that their skills and talents could produce good in the world. They would go on to radically change the outlook of Dublin, especially for the workers at Guinness, but they changed a whole city's future in the process. You see that, through the Guinness line, great men didn't just

---

[198] Mansfield, Stephen. *The Search for God and Guinness: A Biography of the Beer that Changed the World* (Nashville, TN: Thomas Nelson, 2009), p. 59.
[199] Ibid., p. 87.

happen. They were given the support, trust, knowledge, and experience of the older generation so that they could excel and continue the good work God had blessed them with. They exemplified what many fathers today are attempting to do: teach their children quality lessons.

The only problem is that many times fathers today forget the key components: time and energy. The Guinness men had plenty of patience to pass on these traits. Worship for this family moved beyond singing and oozed out of their very lives. Everything they did emerged through an understanding of the blessing and grace God had given them. That is why the first aspect to "The Guinness Way" is discerning the ways of God for life and business.

> We know from his own words that the second Arthur asked these questions of his life and even those that followed him and who were not as passionate about their faith nevertheless tried to understand their lives in terms of a purpose God might be fulfilling in their time.[200]

We can learn many things from their story, but there is one driving force that we cannot overlook. They teach us how we can practically worship God every day. What do you worship God with? Your life!

The hard part for many of us is grasping this idea of worship going beyond singing. In churches all over the world, as soon as the worship band gets up on the stage the rest of the church is asked to stand up and enter into a time of worship. However, many times the worship pastor is not

---

[200] Ibid., p. 255.

the first person we see on a Sunday morning. Worship, to God, begins the moment we wake up. It continues as we eat breakfast, make our way to church, and enter the house of God. Just as worship begins before entering church, it does not end the moment we sit down and stop singing. It continues throughout Sunday morning into the prayers, through the reading of Scripture, moving into and beyond the words of the sermon and right into the fellowship we enjoy with our friends and church families after the service. Worshiping God is not twenty minutes of singing, one day per week; it is an all-day, everyday lifting up of our lives to our God.

That being said, if we cannot take the time to worship God one hour a week in community, how can we worship God privately seven days a week? Dick Staub writes, in *The Culturally Savvy Christian*, that worship and bowing down to God is an essential part of our ability to recognize that we need to step back from the conformities of this world and reconnect with the will of God.

> Privately, publicly, and communally, we practice the disciplines of Jesus to renew our minds, and as our minds are refreshed and restored, we find ourselves resisting the negative force of conformity to the world while experiencing the joy that comes through knowing and doing God's will.[201]

---

[201] Staub, Dick. *The Culturally Savvy Christian: A Manifesto for Deepening Faith and Enriching Popular Culture in an Age of Christianity-Lite* (San Francisco, CA: Jossey-Bass, 2007), pp. 107-108.

Think about Thomas' reaction when Jesus came to him and placed Thomas' hands in and on his wounds. Thomas responded by saying, *"My Master! My God!"* (John 20:28) At that moment, everything Thomas thought he knew about the world, death, and his worldview was crushed. He bowed down in amazement to what was before him by exclaiming that God is beyond everything in this world.

How often do you stop and exclaim, "My Master! My God!"—just like Thomas?

Chris Tomlin, one of the most recognizable figures in worship music, writes:

> It would be so much easier if Paul had used "songs" instead of "bodies." Or maybe "events" or "Sunday mornings" or… "Bodies" is such an encompassing word. This definition requires our mind, heart, soul and strength—our entire lives! And that's just what worship calls for, all of who we are. Any less would not be worship.[202]

The reference to Paul, in this instance, is found in Romans 12:

> So here's what I want you to do, God helping you: Take your everyday, ordinary life—your sleeping, eating, going-to-work, and walking-around life—and place it before God as an

[202] Tomlin, Chris, "Articles: Whispers of Worship," *Royal York Baptist Church*, June 15, 2009,
http://www.royalyorkbaptist.com/index.cfm?i=8011&mid=12&id=17017 (accessed March 10, 2010).

offering. Embracing what God does for you is the best thing you can do for him. (Romans 12:1)

Chris Tomlin ends his article by calling out a new generation, a generation that will take worship away from a solitary understanding of music into our all-around life.

> But I see new generations rising up with a burning flame inside to live out lives of surrender, of sacrifice, of worship to God. The Passion movement is a passage of scripture that best defines this abandon lifestyle. Isaiah 26:8 says, *"Yes, Lord walking in the ways of your truth, we wait eagerly for you; your name and renown are the desire of our souls."* This is not a one-stop deal, but a never-ending life theme, a life that stands in view of the mercy of God and echoes the psalm, *"better is one day in your courts than a thousand elsewhere; I would rather be a doorkeeper in the house of my God than dwell in the tents of the wicked."*[203]

Like I said earlier, what do you worship God with? Your life!

One of my favourite verses on worship is found in the book of Hebrews.

> So let's do it—full of belief, confident that we're presentable inside and out. Let's keep a firm grip on the promises that keep us going. He always keeps his word. Let's see how inventive we can be in encouraging love and helping out, not

---

[203] Ibid.

> avoiding worshiping together as some do but
> spurring each other on, especially as we see the
> big Day approaching. (Hebrews 10:22–25)

I like this verse for a couple of reasons. First, for its encouragement to worship together with others, and secondly, it asks us to look at why we are worshiping. Is it God we are worshiping, or are we just giving him lip service? In other words, are we worshiping only when we have to, or when we think others are watching? Maybe it is the other way around. Maybe we are not worshipping because others are watching us, making us feel uncomfortable. This feeling usually comes during moments of singing worship, but we can be encouraged that it is our heart, not our voice, that we worship God with.

Robin Mark, the composer of many worship songs (like "Days of Elijah," for example, and I strongly recommend looking up the lyrics), puts the heart of worship not in the words he writes but within the heart of the worshipper.

> No matter how foolish and simple our actions, if
> it flows on the fullness, truthfulness, sacrifice and
> passion of the worshipping heart, it will surely
> exceed the most complex and well-crafted praise
> symphony that man could ever create. It may
> even exceed the greatest sacrificial giving that
> man could make in life. It has **everything** to do
> with your **heart** and **little** to do with your
> **practice**![204]

---

[204] Mark, Robin. *Warrior Poets of the 21st Century: A Biblical and Personal Journey in Worship* (Belfast: Ambassador-Emerald, Intl., 2007), p. 192. Emphasis mine.

Worship becomes all about our heart and mindset. Are we too focused on ourselves to worship God? Are we too focused on the people around us or how we are actually worshiping? God tells us that it is within our hearts and minds that we worship him, so the how-tos and the what-withs of worship become obsolete.

Have a look at some of the other verses that speak of worship. Read them and evaluate what they say. I hope you don't just read these verses and say, "Yep, it says to worship God." I would love for you to be able to read these words and ask yourself what God is saying to you about worshipping him. Maybe you are like me while I was growing up and did not like singing in public. It was because of that feeling that I struggled with the concept of worship and what it truly was. I didn't understand worship until I understood that it is our thoughts and hearts that are the center of worship. Have a read through some of these scriptures:

> MATTHEW 4:10, PSALMS 95:6, MATTHEW 15:8–9, REVELATION 4, REVELATIONS 5:10–12, JOHN 4:23–24, JOHN 14:17, PSALMS 37:4, MARK 12:30, PSALMS 96:1–2, PSALMS 47:6, EPHESIANS 5:18–19, COLOSSIANS 3:16, ZEPHANIAH 3:17, MATTHEW 26:30, HEBREWS 2:12, PSALMS 22:22, PSALMS 147:1, DEUTERONOMY 31:21, 1 SAMUEL 16:23, MATTHEW 11:17, PSALMS 33:2–3, PSALMS 81:2, PSALMS 150, LUKE 10:41–42, MATTHEW 18:20, MARK 7:6–7, ISAIAH 29:13, EXODUS 20:3, DEUTERONOMY 5:7, DEUTERONOMY 6:13,

> LUKE 4:8, ACTS 10:26, ACTS 14:15,
> COLOSSIANS 2:18, REVELATION 22:8,
> JEREMIAH 26:2, JOB 1:5, EZRA 3:10–13, PSALMS
> 29:2, PSALMS 42:4, ISAIAH 12:5–6,
> HOSEA 6:6, PHILIPPIANS 3:3, 1 PETER 2:5,
> AND REVELATIONS 19:10.

I will leave you with the words of Amos, a personal favourite of mine.

> At God's coming we face hard reality, not
>   fantasy—
> a black cloud with no silver lining.
>
> I can't stand your religious meetings.
> I'm fed up with your conferences and
>   conventions.
>
> I want nothing to do with your religion projects,
> your pretentious slogans and goals.
>
> I'm sick of your fund-raising schemes,
> your public relations and image making.
>
> I've had all I can take of your noisy ego-music.
> When was the last time you sang to me?
>
> Do you know what I want?
> I want justice—oceans of it.
> I want fairness—rivers of it.
> That's what I want. That's all I want.
>
> Didn't you, dear family of Israel, worship me
> faithfully for forty years in the wilderness,

bringing the sacrifices and offerings I
commanded? How is it you've stooped to
dragging gimcrack statues of your so-called
rulers around, hauling the cheap images of all
your star-gods here and there? Since you like
them so much, you can take them with you when
I drive you into exile beyond Damascus. (Amos
5:20–27)

God doesn't want worship from us that's just lip service. One key way to ensure that we aren't just providing God with lip service is to actually think through the lyrics we sing. We should be singing words that we believe are true, that are accurate depictions of our own lives.

Do we worship God with the same love, adoration, and obedience that our worship songs are calling us to? Or are they just words on a screen that we blindly sing and follow along to? God requires something far greater. The fact is, he doesn't just require true worship; he deserves it. He deserves our whole lives, not just simple words we read once a week.

What is true worship? Your life!

Here is a practical idea for the spiritual discipline of worship.

- Stop referring to Sunday's music time as "entering into worship." You should already be in a place of worship.

And some helpful resources:

- *Warrior Poets of the 21st Century*, by Robin Mark (Greenville, SC: Ambassador International, 2007)
- *Prayer and Worship*, by Kara Powell. (Ventura, CA: Gospel Light, 2009)
- www.worshiptraining.com
- www.worshipdevotional.com

Prayer

> One of the great uses of Twitter and Facebook will be to prove at the Last Day that prayerlessness was not from lack of time.[205]

These strong words from John Piper talk about the lack of prayer life some of us have. Creating a strong relationship takes time, and let's be honest about where the majority of our time gets spent. Is it in prayer, or is it being spent connecting through social media? I'm not saying social media isn't a good use of our time; I'm only suggesting that we should start to look at the way we manage our time.

If we're truly going to make a change in this world, we need to be able to communicate with the one who is guiding us. Prayer is just that—a connection with God. Prayer becomes our way to talk with God about our personal ups and downs as we experience them. Think about this: who do you trust the most in your life right now? It may be God, but it may also be your best friend,

---

[205] Twitter. "John Piper," http://twitter.com/JohnPiper/status/5027319857 (accessed April 2, 2011).

boy/girlfriend, parents, or sibling. Once you have identified that, ask yourself another question: why do you trust that person the most?

More than likely it is because that is the one person you have an open, two-way relationship with. They are probably the person you talk to most and the one you run and tell the moment that cute guy or girl asked you out. They are the one who spends time with you when the world comes crashing down around you.

God wants to be that person and we can communicate that openly and freely with him. The most effective way to do this is through our prayer life. The words Jesus spoke to us throughout the Bible are very clear about our prayer life and the benefits that come from having open communication with God. Have a look at these words from Luke's gospel:

> Here's what I'm saying:
> Ask and you'll get;
> Seek and you'll find;
> Knock and the door will open.
> (Luke 11:9)

Jesus tells us on more than one occasion that he expects us to pray and communicate with him. For one reason or another, we have forgotten this. A huge stumbling block for many of us is that we can't humble ourselves enough to say that we need help.

Jurgen Moltmann, the great German theologian, says,

> Strong men often think that praying is something
> for old women who have nothing left to them
> but the rosary or the hymnbook. It has become
> rather unknown that praying has to do with
> awakening, watching, attention, and the
> expectation of life.[206]

When we look at these words—awakening, watching, attention, and expectation—prayer becomes an active practice. Prayer has a distinct, active relationship and life of its own. In fact, it becomes the first step in moving beyond our own expectations; it becomes our first step towards living a simple and sacrificial life that's unlike anything this world has to offer.

> What are we seeking when we pray? When we
> pray, we are seeking the reality of God, and are
> breaking out of the Hall of Mirrors of our own
> wishes and illusions, in which we are imprisoned.
> That means that when we wake up out of the
> petrifications and numbness of our feelings. If in
> prayer we seek the reality of God's world—
> remember the first line of the "Our Father"
> prayer: "hallowed by thy name, thy
> Kingdom..."—then that is the exact opposite of
> the "opium of the people." Prayer is more like
> the beginning of a cure for the numbing
> addictions of this world.[207]

---

[206] Alston, Wallace M., Michael Welker, and Cynthia A. Jarvis. *Loving God with Our Minds: The Pastor as Theologian—Essays in Honor of Wallace M. Alston.* (Grand Rapids, MI: W.B. Eerdmans Publishers, 2004), p. 195.
[207] Ibid., p. 198.

The question being asked in the "Hall of Mirrors" is this: where are you going for the fulfillment of your dreams? Are you asking the magic mirror of Disney and fairy tale fame, or are you turning to God in complete and utter submission to his will?

Prayer is an active communication that speaks of our trust in him. Matthew 6 gives us more direct words from Jesus about his expectations when it comes to prayer.

> Here's what I want you to do: Find a quiet, secluded place so you won't be tempted to role-play before God. Just be there as simply and honestly as you can manage. The focus will shift from you to God, and you will begin to sense his grace.
>
> The world is full of so-called prayer warriors who are prayer-ignorant. They're full of formulas and programs and advice, peddling techniques for getting what you want from God. Don't fall for that nonsense. This is your Father you are dealing with, and he knows better than you what you need...
>
> In prayer there is a connection between what God does and what you do. You can't get forgiveness from God, for instance, without also forgiving others. If you refuse to do your part, you cut yourself off from God's part.
>
> When you practice some appetite-denying discipline to better concentrate on God, don't make a production out of it. It might turn you into a small-time celebrity but it won't make you a saint. (Matthew 6:6–7, 14–16)

God establishes that the connection between him and us goes beyond mere words. Our expectations of God need to be in line with what he expects of us. He expects us to be like him and forgive, just like he forgave us, to love like he loved us and to live like he lived. Prayer is a connection that goes much deeper than words. It is a connection with all of creation.

> People who thank God every morning for the new day in their lives, people who praise God through their delight in existence and glorify him through their love of life, are not doing something singular. They are only doing what all creatures do, universally and unceasingly, each in its own way. With the lives they live, these people are joining in with the cosmic resonance of God's goodness and beauty. To pray like this means waking up out of the mute world of modernity and turning back to the cosmic solidarity of all created being. Praying means coming awake. So praying means awakening all the senses.[208]

Prayer awakens us to the active connection we have with God every day. It's like saying, "Yes, God. I see you in my life. I see you in the simple everyday tasks." It is an acknowledgement that God is evident all throughout his creation. As leaders, I think this is something we need to do more of. I think we need to be influencing the lives of our

---

[208] Moltmann, Jurgen. "Praying and Watching," www.ptsem.edu/iym/lectures/1999/Moltmann-Praying.pdf (accessed November 26, 2010).

young people by having active prayer lives which give thanks to God, even in the small areas.

What have you stopped thanking God for?

If Jesus expects us to pray, why do so many of us struggle with doing it with regularity and humility? Perhaps we don't see our need for prayer because we have a high view of ourselves and a low view of God.[209] Have we become so prideful that we think we are bigger than God? Do we rely solely on our own financial security? What happens when our pride gets us into trouble? What happens when our pockets run dry? God tells us what he expects us to do—pray. He is waiting to answer.

What should we pray about? How do we pray?

Here are two very important questions we often overlook due to their simplicity: Do you talk to your friends? How do you talk to them? The answer is simple— you just do. There's your answer on how you pray—you just do.

Kary Oberbrunner, in *The Fine Line*, explains,

> Pray honestly. What's on your mind right now? Are you hurting? Tell God about it, and allow His presence to start the healing. Are you afraid? Unload on Him, and you'll feel a lot lighter. Are you battling with doubts? Dump them on God, and you'll be surprised at the peace. Do you feel like God isn't being fair? Tell Him. Don't hold back. He can handle it. God wants you to be

---

[209] Guinness, Os. *The Call: Finding and Fulfilling the Central Purpose of Your Life* (Nashville, TN: W Publishing Group, 1998), p. 106.

> truthful with Him. Let it rip. Give Him your whole
> heart.[210]

Do you talk to your friends everyday? I am going to guess the answer to that question is, "Of course." What about God? Do you speak to him everyday? I am going to challenge you to something right now. I want you to memorize a verse from the Bible to help you remember to speak to God everyday. Are you ready? Here it is, from 1 Thessalonians 5:17—

> Pray continually. (NIV)

Pretty easy, eh? What can you pray about continually? Everything.
Try these:

- Pray for your pastors and youth leaders.
- Pray for each other.
- Pray for the billion people who at this moment do not have clean drinking water.
- Find a book on different countries and pick countries to pray for.
- Pray for the numerous wars that are happening around the world.
- Pray for the First Nations people in Canada.
- Pray for the single mothers in Canada.

---

[210] Oberbrunner, Kary. *The Fine Line: Re-Envisioning the Gap Between Christ and Culture* (Grand Rapids, MI: Zondervan, 2008), p. 88.

- Pray that fathers will grow up and start being the godly men they are called to be.
- Pray for issues of justice (sex trafficking, water, AIDS, food, fair trade, child labour).
- Pray for the white elephant in the room—same-gender attraction.

That is just a small portion of my list, but my point is this—pray about what is important in your life. If it is important to us, it is important to God, and he would love to hear from us. That gives us everything we need to live out 1 Thessalonians 5:17 every day for the rest of our lives. That will keep us thanking God for who he is and what he has done. So, how do we pray? We pray.

Here are some key verses on prayer that can help answer some of the questions we have been working through:

> 1 CORINTHIANS 14:15, MATTHEW 14:23, ACTS 1:14, EPHESIANS 1:16, 1 PETER 3:7, ISAIAH 38:2, LUKE 17:1, PSALMS 42:8, ACTS 4:31, PHILIPPIANS 1:4, MARK 14:39, ROMANS 1:10, MARK 9:29, JEREMIAH 42:4, JOHN 2:1, 1 CORINTHIANS 7:5, LUKE 2:37, 1 THESSALONIANS 5:17, PSALMS 39:12, PSALMS 88:2, JEREMIAH 29:12, MATTHEW 5:44, PSALMS 109:4, 1 THESSALONIANS 3:10, MARK 6:46, LUKE 6:12, ACTS 6:4, DANIEL 6:11, JUDE 1:20, MATTHEW 19:13, MARK 1:35, PSALMS 66:19, ROMANS 12:12, ISAIAH 37:15, COLOSSIANS 1:3, PSALMS 102:17, LUKE 11:2, DANIEL 6:10, 1 TIMOTHY 2:8, JEREMIAH 29:7, PSALMS 86:6, 1

> PETER 3:12, MATTHEW 6:5–9, MATTHEW
> 21:13, LUKE 5:16, ACTS 9:40, ACTS 13:3,
> PSALMS 17:6, HEBREWS 13:18, HEBREWS 5:7,
> REVELATION 8:4, LUKE 1:13, PSALMS 122:6,
> MARK 11:24, AND JAMES 5:15.

After reading some of these verses on prayer, try incorporating this prayer into your daily life. It comes from Sir Francis Drake (1540–1596):

> Disturb us, Lord, when we are too well pleased with ourselves. When our dreams have come true because we dreamed too little. When we arrive safely because we have sailed too close to the shore. Disturb us, Lord.[211]

What are some things in your life that have become comfortable? What are the gifts God has placed in your life that you have stopped thanking him for? Have we started to take the good things in our lives for granted?

Drake asks God to disturb our lives when they become too comfortable, but why does that thought discomfort us? Do we not trust God enough? Do we worry that he won't provide for us when we encounter something that makes us uncomfortable? These uncomfortable moments are exactly the things God wants us to bring to him in prayer. We have been given the amazing gift of relationship with our Saviour, and that includes both the comfortable and uncomfortableness of life.

---

[211] Groeschel, Craig. *Chazown: A Different Way to See Your Life* (Sisters, OR: Multnomah Publishers, 2006), p. 26.

Here are some practical ideas:

- Have a conversation with God.
- Use Google Docs, or any other note-taking app, to keep an active prayer list you can access from anywhere.

And now some helpful resources to go along with the above:

- *Prayer: The Timeless Secret of High Impact Leaders*, by Dave Earley (Chattanooga, TN: Living Ink Books, 2008)
- *Prayer: Finding the Heart's True Home*, by Richard Foster, an audio CD.
- *The Sacred Ways*, by Tony Jones (Grand Rapids, MI: Zondervan, 2005)

Fasting

What does it mean to fast?

The most common answer would probably be not eating for a prolonged period of time, but is that really what fasting means? Many of us, as soon as we hear the word fast, automatically think of events like the 30-Hour Famine, or giving up chocolate for Lent, but have we ever taken the time to hear what God tells us about true fasting? Read Isaiah 58.

> This is the kind of fast day I'm after: to break the
> chains of injustice, get rid of exploitation in the
> workplace, free the oppressed, cancel debts.
> What I'm interested in seeing you do is: sharing
> your food with the hungry, inviting the homeless
> poor into your homes, putting clothes on the
> shivering ill-clad, being available to your own
> families. Do this and the lights will turn on, and
> your lives will turn around at once. (Isaiah 58:6–7)

It sounds as if fasting in God's eyes goes well beyond not eating for a couple of days. When we read the words of Isaiah, fasting becomes less about abstinence from food and more about becoming closer to the will of God. When we enter into a time of fasting, we are choosing to put something aside to grow closer to God. So why do we not bless others with what we are abstaining from?

The Bible, however, only mentions food-type fasting. Mark Driscoll explains how fasting could be applied to other areas of our lives:

> Fasting is the voluntary act of abstaining from
> something for the purpose of growing in self-
> discipline, which is the essence of what it means
> to be a disciple of Jesus Christ. Perhaps the most
> common form of fasting is from food. This is
> because, as Paul says, for some people their
> stomach is their god. By fasting from food, they
> are learning to enjoy food as a gift from God

without allowing it to become an idolatrous
functional god that controls them.[212]

We need to start looking at the little things in our lives
we take for granted which take over our lives. These things
can affect many areas of our lives, especially when it comes
to our media influences. In the same way Paul warns about
gluttony when it comes to food, we need to look at how
much influence we are giving to the media that enters our
lives. Fasting, however, only works if it is a voluntary act.

If fasting is not a voluntary act, undertaken so that we
can get closer to God, it becomes nothing more than the
latest South Beach Diet.

> It is Christian, for fasting by a non-Christian
> obtains no eternal value because the Discipline's
> motives and purposes are to be God-centered. It
> is voluntary in that fasting is not to be coerced.
> Fasting is more than just the ultimate crash diet
> for the body; it is the abstinence from food for
> spiritual purposes... the voluntary denial of a
> normal function for the sake of intense spiritual
> activity.[213]

That is why fasting needs to be voluntary in order to be
successful. It needs to bring us into spiritual growth and
understanding, and only we can choose to do that. The best
way to understand fasting is by reading about it, and the

---

[212] Driscoll, Mark. "Spiritual Disciplines: Fasting," *The Resurgence*,
http://theresurgence.com/Spiritual_Disciplines_Fasting (accessed June 6,
2010).
[213] Whitney, Donald S. *Spiritual Disciplines for the Christian Life* (Colorado
Springs, CO: NavPress, 1991), p. 160.

best place to read about it is the Bible. Jesus is very clear that he expects us to fast, just like he expects us to pray.

> When you practice some appetite-denying discipline to better concentrate on God, don't make a production out of it. It might turn you into a small-time celebrity but it won't make you a saint. If you 'go into training' inwardly, act normal outwardly. Shampoo and comb your hair, brush your teeth, wash your face. (Matthew 6:16–17)

In the same passage, Jesus tells us what to do and not do when it comes to fasting, but throughout the Bible we are given all types and lengths of fasting.

Matthew 4:2 and Luke 4:2 tell of Jesus entering into what we would recognize as a regular abstinence of food as he entered the dessert. He did drink water during this fast, though, unlike the fast in Ezra 10:6 which includes abstaining from water. Daniel entered into a partial fast of eating only vegetables (Daniel 1:12). There are even two instances in the Bible where fasting can only be done with the divine calling of God (Deuteronomy 9:9 and 1 Kings 19:8). Other than telling us that we must engage in fasting, the Bible does not tell us how to fast, or for how long we are to do it.

There are tons of verses that describe different types and lengths of fasts, because the how–long and what-we-fast-from is not the most important aspect to keep in mind. The importance is found in the outcome of our fast. Outcomes can include greater guidance from God, more concentrated prayer, a display of humbleness, delivery from the things that keep us from getting close to God, worshiping God... and those are only a few of the positive aspects that come from entering into periods of fasting. The fast is about God, not us. We need to leave our pride where we left our food—behind us.

Read some of these verses which teach about fasting. See how many variations of fasting there are.

> MATTHEW 3:4, ESTHER 4:16, ACTS 9:9, MATTHEW 6:16–18, JOEL 2:15–16, ACTS 13:2, 2 CHRONICLES 20:3, NEHEMIAH 9:1, JONAH 3:5–8, LEVITICUS 16:29–31, ZECHARIAH 8:19, LUKE 18:12, MATTHEW 9:14–15, JUDGES 20:26, 1 SAMUEL 7:6, 2 SAMUEL 1:12, 3:35, JEREMIAH 36:6, DANIEL 6:18–24, 1 SAMUEL 31:13, 2 SAMUEL 12:16–23, ACTS 27:33–34, DANIEL 10:3–13, 1 KINGS 19:8, LUKE 2:37, ACTS 13:2, ACTS 14:2–3, NEHEMIAH 1:4, EZRA 8:23, AND JOEL 2:12.

Here are some practical ideas for imputing the spiritual discipline of fasting in your life, or into the lives of the youth around you.

- Take part in the 30-Hour Famine, by World Vision.
- Fast for a day from some of these suggestions:
  - o   TV (try for a week).
  - o   Your smart phone.
  - o   Junk food.

- o Caffeine.
- o Social media.

And now some helpful resources:

- *A Hunger for God*, by John Piper (Wheaton, IL: Crossway, 1997)
- *Fasting: The Ancient Practices*, by Scot McKnight and Phyllis Tickle (Nashville, TN: Thomas Nelson, 2009)

Study

Have you read your Bible from cover to cover?

Do you pick up your Bible on any other day besides Sunday?

If you answered "No," you would be just like 80% of the other Christians out there. That is why I talk and write about study. If you told me there was some faith group in the world in which only 80% read their holy book once a week, I would think it was a joke.

Wait a second... that's us.

Let me explain something about statistics for a minute. You can make statistics say anything you want; they present a bent line. You can bend and use them to prove any point you like. That being said, let's move past the 80% statistic. How often do you listen to music? How often do you go on your computer, play video games, or watch TV? If you said everyday, you are probably like me.

Now, how often do you read your Bible? Is it everyday? Is it as often as you watch TV or listen to music? The point is that if you are not reading your Bible, you have to ask yourself where your instructions for living life are coming from. Everybody needs to be reading their Bible everyday. A statistic on this matter should not exist because everyone should be doing it. Statistics are used to prove points, and I don't care what the stat is—whether it is 80% or 20%—because there is no reason we should not be engaging the Scriptures daily. I don't care what books you have read... you need to come back to the source. The source is the Scripture.

I was twenty-six when I first read the Bible cover to cover. I would read parts of it over and over again. We need to be reading the Bible on an ongoing basis as the church, as community, and as individuals. Rob Bell writes, "The Bible tells a story. A story that isn't over. A story that is still being told. A story that we have a part to play in."[214] If the Bible is this grand, overarching meta-narrative that we talked about earlier, would it not be important for us to read the Bible in order, front to back, at least once? I do not know too many experts on Shakespeare who pick and choose which sections of his plays to read. Especially before reading it in completion first.

How many novels, resource books, or ebooks have you read in the past five years?

If it's more than the number of times you've read your Bible, how can you expect to live out the words of Jesus?

---

[214] Bell, Rob. *Velvet Elvis: Repainting the Christian Faith* (Grand Rapids, MI: Zondervan, 2005), p. 66.

We have to study the words of Jesus so that we can actively live out our roles in his grand story. First, however, we need to study the whole story.

How do you study the Bible?

You crack open the Bible and you read it. Did you know there is an app for that? Lots of them! Studying the Bible can be done anywhere, at any time, by anyone... as long as we are willing. There is also a wonderful website where you can read the Bible—www.youversion.com. On that website is a daily reading. I challenge everyone to get on that website and read it daily. YouVersion is striving to make our ancient faith and modern world connect with relevance through community reading.

> We aren't just building a tool to impact the world using innovative technology. More importantly, we are engaging people into relationships with God as they discover the relevance the Bible has for their lives.[215]

Would it not be interesting if we got the churches we attend to read it together? YouVersion allows its users to choose different reading plans depending on their interests and how long they would like to participate, through customizable options. You can read the New Testament, Old Testament, single books, or even find reading plans centered around the chronological breakdown of events in the Bible.

---

[215] YouVersion, "About," http://www.youversion.com/about (accessed August 10, 2010).

Have you ever wondered what it would have
been like to read the Old Testament in ancient
Israel? Or, the New Testament as the books
were written? In this plan, the order of the Old
Testament readings is very similar to Israel's
Hebrew Bible, progressing from Law to Prophets
to Writings. The New Testament ordering is
based upon research regarding the order in
which the books were authored. Although this
research is not conclusive, it may offer helpful
insights to your Bible reading.[216]

YouVersion's simplistic and customizable options allow
readers to engage the Bible where they are, whether it is at
home, in the office, or on the go with their applications.
Imagine if your whole church was reading the same passage
together everyday—at their homes, on the subway, as
families. Imagine the growth and conversations that would
stem from that experience. We could say, "I am reading
Ecclesiastes and so are you, and you, and you," and on and
on it would go. At that point, we could say, "What is God
saying to all of us?"

You might be asking yourself, "Why do we need to
seek solitude, fast, or even pray? God knows I think about
him."

That is true. God knows you think about him, but the
question I would ask you is, how *often* do you think about
him? All these disciplines are difficult and take time to fully
master, but the Bible is very clear that God blesses us when
we enter into times of spiritual growth. God becomes more

than just a name, someone who we believe in when we enter into these practices. God becomes personal to each one of us as we trust him with the intimate details of our lives. When we pray, we trust him to hear us. When we fast, we trust he will be with us and give us strength. When we worship, we are showing him that he is worthy of our praise.

Think about this for a second. If you just met me and I told you I was a football player, after you got over meeting a professional athlete, you would probably ask me a variation of questions—like, "Where do you play?" If my response was an awkward and quiet, "I don't really play anywhere, unless you count my backyard," after you finished laughing you would probably say something along the lines of, "You are a liar." I wouldn't be much of a football player, would I? The same mentality can be taken when it comes to these practices as well. If we do not actively participate in a two-way relationship with God, in which we trust him completely, what kind of Christians are we? Are we just giving God lip service?

There are two questions we have to ask ourselves if all these practices are not part of our lives:

1. Do you know Jesus of Nazareth?
2. Do you know church, structure, and religion?

I could care less if anyone ever met church, structure, and religion. What do I mean by that? Well, I'll give you an example. One time I went to a church where I was the preacher for the night because the pastor was away. I came in and set up on my own, without anyone speaking to me. I sat in a pew off to the side and, again, no one talked to me. As we started singing songs of worship, I got a tap on the shoulder. I was thinking that a leader from the church was about to introduce himself to me, but I could not have been more wrong.

"Excuse me, son, you are in my pew."

I actually smiled, because that had never happened to me before, but I had heard about it, so I gave him his pew. The reality is that when our churches get full, each and every one of us needs to make sure that we are not turning away someone from outside our church. Instead, give them your seat. It is not about us. If these types of things do not start to matter, we need to ask ourselves, what do we really know? When we engage in an active faith, we can learn how to take our faith and transform the culture that surrounds us. Culture can only be transformed by active followers of Christ because our faith penetrates out from our actions and has a greater impact than mere words could ever have.

Here are some practical ideas and some helpful resources for the spiritual discipline of study.

- Read your Bible.
- Use reading plans like *YouVersion* (www.youversion.com).

Here are some helpful resources you can use:

- *Life With God: Reading the Bible for Spiritual Transformation*, by Richard Foster (New York, NY: HarperOne, 2008)
- *Velvet Elvis*, by Rob Bell (Grand Rapids, MI: Zondervan, 2005)
- *Eat This Book: A Conversation in the Art of Spiritual Reading*, by Eugene H. Peterson (Grand Rapids, MI: W.B. Eerdmans Publishing, 2006)

CULTURE

culture

"There is no withdrawing from culture. Culture is inescapable. And that's a good thing."[217]

What is our response to culture? What is our responsibility to culture? Well, the Bible talks about a lot of things. It talks about keys and locks. It talks about a small key opening a big door. It talks about leaven and loaves and how a little bit of leaven rises the loaf. It also talks about light and dark.

> All are metaphors of penetration—salt into food, light into darkness, leaven into loaf, keys into lock. Not a lot of salt is needed to flavor and preserve, as long as the salt is rubbed into the food. Nor does it take a great deal of light to dispel darkness, as long as the light is not

---

[217] Crouch, Andy. *Culture Making: Recovering Our Creative Calling* (Downers Grove, IL: InterVarsity Press, 2008), p. 36.

covered. A tiny bit of fermenting yeast can make a whole loaf rise. And a small key can open a great door.[218]

People always say, "Light and darkness... right, I got this. I go to church."

Light Up the Darkness

Wait a second. Let's analyze this a little differently. If I took a Bic lighter and turned off all the lights in the room, you would say, "Light and dark... I get it. Now let's move on." What if I grabbed one of those eighteen million kilowatt bulb flashlights from Costco, the ones that do not even have a button—just a handle. To turn them on, you have to crack the handle down and a beam of light shoots out, making the Bic lighter look pathetic. That is the light we are after.

Is your life a Bic lighter or a beacon of light?

If I were to take that flashlight outside and turn it on, I would be grabbing a buddy and having *Star Wars* lightsaber duels right away. It shoots into the sky, becoming a piercing, blinding, transforming light. That is what we are called to be. If we walk outside with a Bic lighter, how many steps would it take before it disappears? Two? Step... step, gone? That is not the light we are called to be. Those lights are extinguished even before you step foot outside

[218] Ford, Leighton. *Transforming Leadership: Jesus' Way Of Creating Vision, Shaping Values & Empowering Change* (Downers Groove, IL: InterVarsity Press, 1991), p. 67.

your door. How can you ever take your light beyond your front door?

Salt

My favourite analogy is salt. Salt is a preserving agent. In biblical times, you would not get your steaks from your local grocery store; you would get a chunk of meat and rub salt on it to season it. The salt would also stop it from going bad.

I love John Stott, the great evangelist, and I apologize because this is an extremely old school quote. Nonetheless, he says:

> Christian salt [you and me], has no business to remain snugly in elegant ecclesiastical salt cellars; our place is to be rubbed into the secular community, as salt is rubbed into meat, to stop it going bad. And when society does go bad, we Christians tend to throw up our hands in pious horror and reproach to the non-Christian world; but should we not rather reproach ourselves?[219]

The first part of that quote is basically saying: do not leave it on the shelf. *"And when society does goes bad, we Christians tend to throw up our hands in pious horror and reproach to the non-Christian world."* We blame society. However, we should be angry and full of reproach towards ourselves. One can hardly blame unsalted meat for going bad. There is

---

[219] Stott, John. *The Message of the Sermon on the Mount* (Downers Grove, IL: InterVarsity Press, 1985), p. 65.

nothing else it can do but go bad. The better question to ask is, where is the salt?

Where are we? I just do not think we are there.

Bob Briner, in the great book *Roaring Lambs*, says:

> Christians must penetrate areas of culture to have a preserving effect. And penetration does not mean standing outside and lobbing hand grenades of criticism over the wall. It is not about being reactionary and negative. It is about being inside through competence and talent.[220]

Us vs. Them

So here is the tough question. What makes *something* Christian and not *someone* Christian?

Why is Christian music one of the only genres of music on the planet categorized based on somebody's faith and not the genre of music that they sing? I know bands that are Satanic and they are classified as rock. I know bands that are Wiccan and they are classified as punk. Have you ever noticed where we place an artist that is Christian on iTunes? They are labeled under "Inspirational." What does that even mean? When you look at the bottom of the iTunes Inspirational page, you can buy some Zen or Buddhist music. I don't know about you, but other artists inspire me at different points in my day, not to mention my life, depending on what I am going through. Should not they all be labeled inspirational? Why can I not buy my Jay-Z or

---

[220] Briner, Bob. *Roaring Lambs: A Gentle Plan to Radically Change Your World* (Grand Rapids, MI: Zondervan Publishing House, 2000), p. 40.

Lights tracks on the same page where I buy my Chris Tomlin or Group 1 Crew tunes?

When we created this "us vs. them" culture, we created our very own mission field, right across our street.

> The greatest mission field we face is not in some faraway land. The strange and foreign culture most Americans fear is not across the ocean. It's barely across the street. The culture most lost to the gospel is our own—our children and neighbors. It's a culture that can't say two sentences without referencing a TV show or a pop song... It's a culture more likely to have a body part pierced than to know why Sarah laughed. It's a culture that we stopped loving and declared a culture war upon.[221]

I was a teacher for over a decade and people knew I was a Christian because of how I lived, what I said, and what I did. If a band wants to go and leave our Christian world and sing, we have a name for them in mainstream media—they are called crossover artists. Where are they crossing over to? That's right, they are crossing over to where God calls us to be, but we as Christians use it as a negative thing. If I took all the plumbers from my community who knew Christ and created the Christian Plumbers of Greater Durham Region, you would think I was an idiot. Let them plumb where they plumb. Having a special classification for Christian music is a really dumb idea. It is a manmade creation from

---

[221] Staub, Dick. *The Culturally Savvy Christian: A Manifesto for Deepening Faith and Enriching Popular Culture in an Age of Christianity-Lite* (San Francisco, CA: Jossey-Bass, 2007), p. 54. Quoting Dwight Ozard.

the mid-1970s, and to this day we still think it is biblical. But it is not.

We could make a Christian version of virtually anything. They have YouTube, and we have GodTube. They have Guitar Hero, and we have Guitar Praise. The world has Tic-Tacs, and we have Testamints. Then there is my favourite example of all—Twitter and Chirp. They are both bird sounds! We do not need to take something and make separate Christian versions.

What we are doing is not working.

Let's take Christian movies. I think Christian movies are really bad. Let's just leave it at that. Here is a paradigm change. If you are good at language and writing, go to a university with a great journalism program and get yourself a degree. When you graduate, go to Hollywood, Vancouver, or Toronto—wherever they are making movies—and become the head writer, who is a Christian, for *Transformers 3*. Then when someone around that table of writers says, "I have a great idea. Let's talk about masturbation again," you can say no and lean over and tell them to sit down. You are the head writer. Can you picture what the world would look like if a thousand writers, producers, and filmmakers who are Christians descended on Hollywood this year and the years that follow? The world would begin to change.

"Brett, I am not a writer."

That's okay. What are you good at? Use it to change the world. Last year, I was on a plane flying to Alberta and I noticed a guy across the way reading a Shane Claiborne book. In my head, I was thinking, *I know Shane*, and I start to talk to the man reading the book. I asked him his name and he told me it was Mike. I asked him what he did and he said he ran a hockey camp in Ottawa. I thought that was cool. He asked me my name and what I did, so the familiars were all out in the open now. We talked for a bit of the flight. We then got off the flight and were grabbing our luggage when this kid comes running up to him stammering, "M... M... Mike, I am a big fan. Can I have your autograph?"

"Dude, what's your last name?" I ask next. It was Mike Fisher from the Ottawa Senators. Here is a guy living out his life on the ice every night, changing his world. We need to start asking ourselves what we are good at and how we can live that out in the world—not the Christian world or the secular world, but simply the world. There is no sacred, secular divide. If you know Jesus, you are doing secular work no matter what.

How do we discern the culture we live in is a simple process. Start by looking at those top movies, songs, and video games we recorded earlier in the book and ask yourself a couple questions about them:

What is the worldview of the media? How does that compare with a Biblical worldview? What is my response?[222]

This will work with anything. What is Lil' Wayne's worldview when it comes to women? All you need to do is find any video he has ever done and you'll see what it is— you, as a woman, are good for nothing but sex. Then take that and ask, what does the Bible say? The Bible tells me that you are worth much more than that.

---

[222] CPYU.org with Walk Mueller.

The response I would suggest is to choose your God. My pastor, Jon Thompson, has said, "Beneath all of our technology in Canada you will find the average person— educated or uneducated—involved in one or more practices that God says is nothing more than dangerous."[223] Jon then went on to name them off. "Tarot cards, psychic reading, crystals, the new age, witchcraft, horoscopes, outright Satanism, Ouija boards, reincarnation, séances, ghosts, levitation, palm reading, numerology, idols, astrology."[224]

Are these in our world?

My wife and I were shopping at Toys 'R' Us a while ago and my daughter, out of the corner of my eye, picks up this little pink case with a handle on it. I am thinking it is Monopoly Junior for girls. I look over and find that it is an Ouija board. It is at the Kraft Dinner height of any store. You know, that height where any little kid can see it and get excited over the packaging. What is the world saying when we are selling Ouija boards to kids? If there are angels and God, then there are demons and Satan. If you wilfully ask for a demonic presence in your life, I do not even have the time to walk through all the pain you are going to cause.

I go on to add some areas of concern to Jon's list. Sexual practices and sexual immorality (masturbation to porn, sexual movies, affairs). The love of watching extreme violence or torture. Downloading music, movies, or software. Abusing our bodies through drugs, alcohol,

---

[223] Tompson, Jon. "Sermon," in Carruthers Creek Community Church (Ajax, 2010).
[224] Ibid.

gluttony, and lack of exercise. Laziness, busyness, apathy, and lastly—not offering Jesus our sole allegiance but living a blended life.

There is no such thing as a biblical worldview in anything sexual. When we start living in this biblical worldview and lifestyle, we start to become like the conformists we talked about earlier. Our ancient faith starts to become clouded by the modern world as we allow our biblical values to be replaced. It is a biblical worldview, period. We are supposed to be pruning off those unbiblical branches every single day of our lives. It is a battle that will never end, and for some of us it is a battle that hasn't even started. If we are not attempting to win this battle, we do not have sole allegiance to God, but are instead living a blended life.

This is not the final word on the matter. Keep learning, keep searching, and keep reading. I think Yoda might have said it the best, and with the most clarity, when he said, "No. Try not. Do... or do not. There is no try."[225] We all have a choice. Choices to either live a biblical worldview that is in touch with our ancient faith, or a life that is of this world.

> Don't love the world's ways. Don't love the world's goods. Love of the world squeezes out love for the Father. Practically everything that goes on in the world—wanting your own way, wanting everything for yourself, wanting to appear important—has nothing to do with the

---

[225] *Star Wars: Empire Strikes Back*. Directed by Irvin Kershner, Twentieth Century Fox Film Corporation (1980).

> Father. It just isolates you from him. The world
> and all its wanting, wanting, wanting is on the way
> out—but whoever does what God wants is set
> for eternity. (1 John 2:15–17)

Dick Staub creates a mission statement for all culturally engaged Christians. He essentially lays out three elements of our lives that we need to examine if we are going to honestly look at media, faith, and culture.

> For we are called to be culturally savvy
> Christians, who are serious about faith, savvy
> about faith and culture, and skilled at fulfilling
> our calling to be a loving, transforming presence
> in the world.[226]

Is faith important to you?

Is it important enough to lead you to question your decisions about media?

If faith takes a backseat to culture, we are stuck in a biblical worldview mixed with... *(fill in the blank)*. That is not how we are called to live.

> Anyone who sets himself up as "religious" by
> talking a good game is self-deceived. This kind of
> religion is hot air and only hot air. Real religion,
> the kind that passes muster before God the
> Father, is this: Reach out to the homeless and
> loveless in their plight, and guard against

---

[226] Staub, Dick. *The Culturally Savvy Christian: A Manifesto for Deepening Faith and Enriching Popular Culture in an Age of Christianity-Lite* (San Francisco, CA: Jossey-Bass, 2007), p. xv.

corruption from the godless world. (James 1:26–27)

A fully alive life that is culturally relevant can only be attained with a serious grounding in the word of God.

Are we savvy with our faith?

Savvy, by definition, is essentially having knowledge, being informed, and engaging whatever your area of specialty is. In order to have a biblical worldview and an understanding of your ancient faith, you need to achieve a balance of knowledge and application. Too much knowledge and we can become arrogant before the eyes of those we are trying to engage. When this happens, we begin to live like separatists too focused on the rights and wrongs of God's word, causing us to miss the true message behind his life. However, too much desire for worldly involvement leads us into the life of conformists. Being accepted by the world takes precedence over living a life for God. When we reach that balance of knowledge and application, we become true transformists. The world, and the people around us, takes notice of the life we live because it is not about us. It is about Jesus.

> You don't get wormy apples off a healthy tree, nor good apples off a diseased tree. The health of the apple tells the health of the tree. You must begin with your own life-giving lives. It's who you are, not what you say and do, that counts. Your true being brims over into true words and deeds. (Luke 6:43–45)

Do we know the skills needed to fulfill our purpose?

We are all on a journey. We will never know everything. That being said, our understanding of the third challenge lain before us is to stay informed. When we keep ourselves engaged, focused, and motivated, we can be a voice for those who are looking for help.

> So if you're serious about living this new resurrection life with Christ, act like it. Pursue the things over which Christ presides. Don't shuffle along, eyes to the ground, absorbed with the things right in front of you. Look up, and be alert to what is going on around Christ—that's where the action is. See things from his perspective. Your old life is dead. Your new life, which is your real life—even though invisible to spectators—is with Christ in God. He is your life... So, chosen by God for this new life of love, dress in the wardrobe God picked out for you: compassion, kindness, humility, quiet strength, discipline. Be even-tempered, content with second place, quick to forgive an offense. Forgive as quickly and completely as the Master forgave you. And regardless of what else you put on, wear love. It's your basic, all-purpose garment. Never be without it. (Colossians 3:1–3, 12–14)

It is there where we come all the way back to media, faith, and culture. Do you know what people say?

"Where do I start? Considering everything we talked about, where do I even begin?"

Engage Culture

Bill Hybels calls it your holy disconnect; you start with one thing. You start with that one thing that just ate at you as you read the book, the one thing that just wrecked your whole understanding of your life. Whatever wrecks you is what you start with. Maybe it is sexuality. You may be struggling with Internet pornography. You may be struggling with lust. Whatever it is, the first step is being honest with yourselves and those closest to you. Maybe you struggle with self-injury. You might be thinking of suicide daily. You may feel alone and abandoned, but reach out to those around you. The help and support you are looking for could be in the next room. It could be in the Bible on your shelf. You might be looking at your DVD collection and realize that violence has taken over your life.

Maybe the question is, do you know Jesus? Has the worldview of media replaced the God you used to know? I am encouraged by students on a nightly basis because you are the ones who care deeply about justice. You are the ones who are building wells, and I hope nothing stops you from seeking what you are passionate about. I challenge you that if an adult shoots down your idea, or dream, move on to the next one. If that fails, find another person and keep searching. We all look at life through jaded eyes at some point and it is about time we stop telling ourselves we cannot change the world and we got up off our couches and gave it a go.

You have three days. You have three days to make a choice whether what you read in this book is worth it or not. Do not tell me you will try. When you put this book down, when you go to your next movie, when you watch your next music video, or when you listen to your iPod next, you have some serious questions to ask. If after three days you have not started to ask yourself some serious questions, you never will, or at least not until you read these words again. That means all the time, all the energy, and all the thought that goes into a book like this becomes a waste of time. I challenge you not to make it a waste.

At one of my talks this year, I heard a young guy say to his buddies, "I hope he doesn't challenge my pop-cultureness." He was not willing to see past the Lil' Wayne, or *The Hills,* or the Drake worldview to the life worth living. He was stuck in this fake, materialistic world that had become comfortable. But I hope that is not you. I hope you start questioning everything around you like you never have before.

Here are some helpful resources that look at faith and culture:

- Relevant Magazine (www.relevantmagazine.com)
- Neue Magazine (www.neuemagazine.com)
- Risen Magazine (www.risenmagazine.com)
- www.CPYU.org
- Christ and Pop Culture, a blog (www.christandpopculture.com)
- The Next-Wave Blog (www.the-next-wave.info)
- Culture Making, a blog (www.culture-making.com)

- *Download: Teaching Students to Filter Their Choices with Walt Mueller*, a DVD curriculum (http://www.cpyuresourcecenter.org/download -dvd.html)
- *Where Faith and Culture Meet*, a DVD curriculum
- *Culture Making: Recovering Our Creative Calling*, by Andy Crouch (Downers Grove, IL: InterVarsity Press, 2008)
- *UnChristian: What a New Generation Really Thinks about Christianity... and Why it Matters*, by David Kinnaman and Gabe Lyons (Grand Rapids, MI: Baker Books, 2007)

Media

I challenge you when it comes to media to discern it. Do not just buy into everything it says. Start questioning the worldview it promotes.

Faith

I challenge you to dive into your faith like you never have before.

Culture

How do we engage culture as individuals, in our families, and with our friends?

I pray that you leave after reading this book with some discomfort in your heart, some anger in your soul, some tears in your eyes and some foolishness in your life.

> May God bless you with discomfort at easy answers, half-truths, and superficial relationships, so that you may look deep within your heart.
> May God bless you with anger at injustice, oppression, and the exploitation of people, so that you may work for justice, freedom, and peace.
> May God bless you with tears to shed for those who suffer from pain, rejection, starvation, and war, so that you may reach out your hand to comfort and turn their pain into joy.
> And may God bless you with enough foolishness to believe that you can make a difference in this world, so that you can do what others claim cannot be done.[227]

I leave you with the words of Erwin McManus, "If our children are going to walk away from Christ, we need to raise them in such a way that they understand that to walk away from Jesus is to walk away from a life of faith, risk, and adventure and to choose a life that is boring, mundane, and ordinary."[228] I challenge you to present to the youth around you a life that is alive and nothing close to

---

[227] Groeschel, Craig. "May God Bless You With Discomfort: Franciscan Benediction," *Swerve*, September 17, 2007, http://swerve.lifechurch.tv/2007/09/17/may-god-bless-you-with-discomfort/ (accessed August 10, 2010).
[228] McManus, Erwin Raphael. *The Barbarian Way: Unleash the Untamed Faith Within* (Nashville, TN: Thomas Nelson Books, 2005), p. 122.

mundane. I challenge you to a life that reflects the love of Christ and to live based on a strong biblical worldview.

contact me

If you have any questions or would like to talk more to me about anything said in this book you can find me through the contact information below

Email:
brett@brettullman.com

Web:
www.brettullman.com—my speaking site
www.yourstory.info—my self-injury site
www.worldsapart.org—network, empower, and support the Canadian church

Other:
facebook.com/brettullman
twitter.com/brettullman
youtube.com/brettu

key to text-speak test

KOTL: "Kiss on the lips."
AYDY: "Are you done yet?"
CUL8R: "See you later," or "Call you later."
DL: "Down low," or "Download."
NE1: "Anyone."
SLAP: "Sounds like a plan."
TWSS: "That's what she said."
CD9: "Code 9." (Parents are around)
PAL: "Parents are listening."
SOE: "Start of exams."
BIO: "Bring it on."
BBS: "Be back soon."
CYE: "Check your email."
MYO: "Mind your own..."
RYS: "Read your screen."
TTYL: "Talk to you later."

BAG: "Busting a gut."
CU46: "See you for sex."
PRON: "Pornography."
UG2BK: "You've got to be kidding."